BEST
BRITISH
POETRY

2012

◇　◇　◇

SASHA DUGDALE was born in Sussex. She works as a translator and consultant for the Royal Court and other theatre companies. Her translation, *Plasticine* by Vassily Sigarev, won the Evening Standard Award for Most Promising Playwright. She has published two collections of translations of Russian poetry and three collections of her own poetry, *Notebook* (2003), *The Estate* (2007) and *Red House* (2011). In 2003 she received an Eric Gregory Award.

RODDY LUMSDEN (born 1966) is a Scottish poet, who was born in St Andrews. He has published six collections of poetry, a number of chapbooks and a collection of trivia, as well as editing a generational anthology of British and Irish poets of the 1990s and 2000s, *Identity Parade*. He lives in London where he teaches for The Poetry School. He has done editing work on several prize-winning poetry collections and edited the Pilot series of chapbooks by poets under 30 for tall-lighthouse. He is organiser and host of the monthly reading series BroadCast in London. In 2010, he was appointed as Poetry Editor for Salt Publishing.

THE
BEST
BRITISH
POETRY
2012

◇ ◇ ◇

Sasha Dugdale, *Editor*

Roddy Lumsden, *Series Editor*

SALT

CROMER

PUBLISHED BY SALT PUBLISHING
12 Norwich Road, Cromer, Norfolk NR27 0AX United Kingdom

Printed in Great Britain by Clays Ltd, St Ives plc

Typeset in Bembo 10.5 / 12

ISBN 978 1 90773 25 9 paperback

3 5 7 9 8 6 4

CONTENTS

FOREWORD

by Roddy Lumsden

◊　◊　◊

The poems presented in this volume were selected from UK-based poetry magazines, literary journals and online publications issued between spring 2011 and spring 2012. The main purpose of this volume is to celebrate the thriving scene of literary magazines and the developing sphere of literary sites online. For the past year, Sasha Dugdale and I have been reading these publications as they appeared, seeking poems which we felt should be reproduced here. Though I made recommendations, the choices were ultimately up to Sasha, as this year's Guest Editor. The format of the book owes a debt to The Best American Poetry series of anthologies which was founded in 1988. Similar volumes appear each year in Canada, Australia and Ireland. I would like to thank the series editor of BAP, David Lehman for his advice on editing the series. Both Sasha and I would have liked to include Denise Riley's excellent and moving poem 'A Part Song', certainly one of the year's poetic highlights; however the work's length (it consists of twenty sections) was an issue and we did not feel an extract would do it justice.

INTRODUCTION

by Sasha Dugdale

◊ ◊ ◊

Best British Poetry is an anthology of single poems, and in this it is like the celebratory annual Forward Book. One important difference between the two anthologies is that in this book the poets are asked to write a passage about the poem. How they do this is left to them – it can be an astonishingly literal thing, or a piece of poetic prose. This seems to me to be in its own way revolutionary: instead of an editor's introduction, in which the learned editor opines at length on the state of the nation's poetry and presents a few of his chosen poets to reinforce his views, the introduction is divided into seventy or more smaller introductions, each as fascinating as the next, and none presuming to speak on more than the poet actually knows.

The other very attractive quality of this anthology is the ease with which it moves between style, school and generation in order to present a touchingly communal portrait of contemporary poetry. This is particularly striking when you read through the commentaries. It is almost possible to imagine yourself at a very large and amicable poetry symposium, where everyone reads, speaks and listens in turn. Some of these poets live at the corners of the land, others in the centre, some do not travel, others never stand still: the gathering is quite utopian, and yet whilst you read, it does in fact take place.

The poems here were taken from magazines and we made efforts to read as broad a selection of magazines as possible. Magazine editors therefore played a large part in the compilation of this anthology, and as most of their work is 'on-a-shoestring, burning-the-candle-at-both-ends' labour of love, I would like to acknowledge them, their taste and integrity. We took work from some of the more established poetry magazines, like *Poetry Review* and *Poetry London*, but we also took poems from a variety of smaller magazines and online magazines, like *Clinic, 10th Muse, Halfcircle, the Delinquent* and *New Linear Perspectives*. Poetry is a democratic genre, and it is always heartening to witness the plurality of small cultures within the larger poetry scene, and the ways in which poets move between the cultures. There is no sense in imposing any sort of hierarchy on the world of poetry: the smallest magazine, and the least known author, can publish a poem of such revelatory force that it takes its place alongside the greats. But some magazines, like *Poetry London*, manage the feat of publishing a constant stream of excellent and diverse poems and deserve their large following.

A common criticism of contemporary poetry is that it recedes into the personal anecdote and there was a fair amount of poetry in many of the magazines, which displayed this flabby obsession with the details of a life, failing to transform them into anything more than the sum of their parts. Another weakness in some of the poetry we read was an unthinking use of language, resorting to clichés, or misusing idiom inadvertently. I read any number of helpful articles in the magazines over the year, warning would-be writers to avoid such faults, but the basic line is that poetry requires a degree of discipline and an obsessiveness which we do not all possess in equal measure, and many may not be prepared to surrender themselves to its sometimes destructive force.

However, the poems here display no such weaknesses. They are all written by poets at the top of their game, and they deserve the title 'Best British Poetry'. The 'B-word', as Roddy put it in last year's introduction, is no favourite of mine, but take it in the spirit in which it is meant: these are poems worth reading, not the only poems worth reading, but a very good start, if you weren't able to spend, like us, long hours in the Poetry Library last year. A large anthology like this one merely hints at the variety of the scene, rather than placing a deadening stamp of approval on a few poets' foreheads.

The commentaries on the poems are various but they share an extraordinary degree of erudition, of reference to and resonance with the language and the past. This generation, as every generation, depends on the complex past for its voice, and the breadth of style and colour in the poems is matched by an equal breadth of rootwork. Even apparently straightforward narrative and observation, such as the narrative in Patience Agbabi's 'Unfinished Business', is a study of Chaucer and film noir, or Hilary Menos's 'Bob's Dogs' which is a homage to R.S. Thomas's poems. Poetry never exists in a vacuum, we are all constantly in a fine negotiation with the past, but this group of poems seems particularly rich in allusion.

There are other themes and threads which run through the selection, although these may simply be my own preoccupations, and so particularly visible to me. Preeminent amongst these is poetry of place and poetry about specific landscapes. Some of these places, like John Gohorry's Coventry and Andrew Greig's Fife are powerfully particular urban or provincial landscapes, others, like Karen McCarthy Woolf's skilful setting of her Grandfather's London speech or Christine de Luca's Shetlandic 'Discontinuity', are rooted by means of dialect. Some, like Rory Waterman's

'Marstrand', use carefully observed place to unsettling effect. 'A Local Habitation', David Constantine's poem from *The Rialto*, sums up this dedication to locality, the poet is 'ingrown', a love of place so intense that it hurts desperately to remember the place lost. Many of these landscapes themselves, under such exacting scrutiny, assume a mythical shape, they are more than just sodden fields, lanes, waterways, industrial estates – they become for an instant glimpses of promised lands, or lands haunted by the past. Through landscape many of the poems reach out to the old matters of time passing and death.

A final count of poets revealed that this anthology has more women poets than men. I should say that I was not aware of gender balance, and when Roddy and I were choosing poems I often didn't check who had written the poem. Still there is a long history of imbalance in poetry anthologies. *The New Poetry* (1962) appears to have had no British women poets in it, and the first series of *Penguin Modern Poets* included three women out of eighty-one poets, so I don't feel much anguish at our slightly skewed selection.

I was very keen to include the work of some poets who lived and worked in Britain but did not write in English and I was lucky to come across the work of Yang Lian and Amarjit Chandan in translation. Then there was the lyrically rich music of David Morley's Romani version of Lorca's ballad. But there is no doubt that we need to be more aware of the British writers who write in other languages and whose experiences may bring much to our poetic culture. That perhaps is my only request to editors: to actively search out the unheard non-English voices in British poetry. Now that would be a utopian meeting!

We did have a strong sense that the poems we had gathered had a meaningful co-existence as a single volume and said something collectively about the health of British poetry. I can't make any more claims for this little book, although I've read it through a few times now and I see that all the poems have integrity and distinctiveness and that vitality of language which is indicative of the best poetry.

THE
BEST
BRITISH
POETRY

2012

◊　◊　◊

Bees' Nest

◊ ◊ ◊

Bumble-, not honey-; and not a hive.
Ignore those trim little boxes, fitted
with a glass inner lid for viewing
and an entry tunnel of the right gauge,
in friends-of-the-planet catalogues.

Such things may do the trick for blue tits,
with their predictable minds. This bee
won't be invited into your parlour.
She'll build in your compost heap; she'll squat
in a disused mouse-hole; or she's

a cross noise buzzing inside the lawn
so that you desist from using clippers,
and an ever-larger moss-thatched skull
rises from the earth like the Green Man,
his head crowning, being slowly born.

With luck it will be in a summer
rich with visitors, so that a child
may find herself transfixed by a procession
of bees, all in the house uniform,
popping out of the grass, just like that,

to go browsing in the buddleia
or shove their snouts into yellow toadflax,
until they or their clone-kin zoom back
unerringly to the secret trapdoor
that gives access to their waxen dome.

But you worry that you haven't enough
flowers in your garden to feed them,
and that being more rare now they'll never
come back after this year's nest has sagged
into ruin. And they don't come back.

from *Poetry London*

Unfinished Business

◇   ◇   ◇

Conveniently, cowardice and forgiveness look identical at a certain distance. Time steals your nerve. 'Memento Mori', Jonathan Nolan

That night, it rained so hard
it was biblical. The Thames sunk the promenade,
spewing up so much low life.
It's a week since they beat up my wife,
put five holes in my daughter. I know who they are.
I know why. I'm three shots away from the parked car
in a blacked-out car park. My wife cries,
Revenge too sweet attracts flies.
Even blushed with bruises she looks good. She's lying
on the bed, next to me. *Honey, I'm fine.*
Tonight I caught her, hands clasped, kneeling,
still from a crime scene.
I didn't bring my wife to Gravesend for this.
What stops me, cowardice?
None of them, even Joe, has the right to live.
How can I forgive?

How can I forgive
none of them? Even Joe has the right to live.
What stops me, cowardice?
I didn't bring my wife to Gravesend for this
still from a crime scene.
Tonight I caught her, hands clasped, kneeling
on the bed next to me. *Honey, I'm fine.*
Even blushed with bruises she looks good. She's lying.
Revenge too sweet attracts flies
in a blacked-out car park. My wife cries.
I know why. I'm three shots away from the parked car

put five holes in my daughter. I know who they are.
It's a week since they beat up my wife,
spewing up so much low life
it was biblical. The Thames sunk the promenade
that night, it rained so hard.

from *Poetry Review*

TARA BERGIN

Stag-Boy

◊　◊　◊

He enters the carriage with a roar –
he clatters in wildly and fills up the carriages with heat,
running through the train, staining the floor
with hooves dirty from the street;
tearing at the ceilings with his new branched horns,
banging his rough sides against the seats and
the women, who try to look away: Gallant!
He sings hard from his throat,
his young belling tearing at his chest,
pushing at his boy-throat.

Stag-boy –

the train's noise hums in his ears,
sharp and high like crickets pulsing
in the tall grass,
and he wounds it with his horns,
maddened like a stung bull,
pushing up his head,
pushing up his mouth for his mother's teat:
Where is her beestings?
Where is the flowered mug she used to warm his milk in?

No good, no good now.

He's smashing out of the train door,
he's banging his hooves in the industrial air,
he's galloping through the city squares,
and drinking from a vandalised spring –

And still his mother walks through the house,
crying: *Stag-boy, oh stag-boy come home!*

from *Modern Poetry in Translation*

Sow

◊ ◊ ◊

'Dainty footwear turns a young lady into an altogether more beautiful
creature . . .' —*Etiquette for Ladies*, ELIZA SELL

Trottering down the oss road in me new hooves
I'm farmyardy sweet, fresh from the filth
of straw an swill, the trembly-leg sniff
of the slaughter wagon. A guzzler, gilt.
Trollopy an canting. Root yer tongue beneath
me frock an gulp the brute stench of the sty.

I've stopped denying meself: nibbling
grateful as a pet on baby-leaves, afeared
of the glutton of belly an rump. I've sunk
an when lads howd out opples on soft city palms
I guttle an spit, for I need a mon
wi a body like a trough of tumbly slop
to bury me snout in.

All them saft years of hiding at 'ome
then prancing like a pony for some sod to bridle
an shove down the pit, shying away
from 'is dirty fists. All them nights,
me eyes rolling white in the dark when the sow I am
was squailin' an biting to gerrout.

Now no mon dare scupper me,
nor fancy-arse bints, for I've kicked the fence
an I'm riling on me back in the muck,
out of me mind wi gruntin pleasure,

trotters pointing to the heavens like chimdey pots,
stickin V to the cockerel
prissy an crowing on 'is high church spire.

from *Poetry London*

Black Country glossary

oss road: *street*; gilt: *sow*; canting: *cheeky or saucy*; guttle: *chew*;
saft: *foolish*; squalin: *squealing or crying*; bints: *derogatory slang for girls*; riling: *writhing*

8

Roll-on

◊   ◊   ◊

Sweat is not fashionable. My father said
before deodorants, how people stank.
His infant teacher, built like a small tank,
would loom in her stout blouse above his head.
Though honeysuckle blew, the village went
into one private cave of hot, sharp scent.

No one could love the sour reek of the Tube,
its summer greeting, the warm winds of hell.
Some riders walked, until the heatwave fell,
turned bearable. But vans still speed, goods move,
and I am startled when the drivers come
dry-skinned, with aftershave a low, harsh hum.

Horses sweat, men perspire and ladies glow.
But I am drenched, breasts, thighs and thinning skull,
till wind streams over and my body cools.
Earth turns on heat, despite the drugstore's show.
The goods are packed, the stable swept. And I
drink in the rain, which is the sweat of sky.

from *The North*

VAHNI CAPILDEO

Four Departures from 'Wulf and Eadwacer'

◇ ◇ ◇

(i) reverse

It takes nothing from you that I have him –
   Bunched up in your ruins, you cannot lose.

He works alone.

Two sides of one city hide us.
Things fall apart, worked roads recoiling.
   Your lot would siphon grey from graveyards.
   Bunched up in your ruins, you cannot lose.

He works alone.

Near him I narrow to survival mode, wink out;
cannot say the time the place the mood,
hardly the aspect or the gender; again
we did nothing, we did nothing.

Could he for once be nobody's business –
   All too brightly meaningful
   ringbound dossiers flashing their backs,

I reach for the sleep he'd implanted in me;
turn my thorax inside out.

No pen and ink does it justice –
A Stanley knife lullaby score.

(ii) outside

'What was so lacking in the upbringing we gave her that she had to go off with a stranger, one of *them* as well; she's worthless, no getting her back, but so long as they're in touch with each other they're within our reach, for globalisation is also on our side. Their so-called love's as natural-seeming as the rain that falls with bitter charge, entering through the eardrums of our not-so-young houses to ancestral designs *he* only hopes to repossess. She's torn – it is transparent – about throwing in her lot with a fancy-passport foreigner whose hyena ways must make her sick. Best not lose sleep over prayers that her bastard will self-destruct in the womb, taking the mother to some lesser mansion in Heaven; never forget she is one of us, after all. A satisfactory solution will be found.'

(iii) inside

If the present could be bloodier – can't imagine how.

Dear Lord, I never intended this.

You were one kind of invasion, and another,
and it won't stop raining.

'I gave us all up?' To him. For him.

Dear Lord, I never intended this.

We made notes only in mud or on pieces of wood
for burning, burnt; for cementing, trampled.
What can you hope to recover?
The nightjar stuck in my throat?

(iv) alpha@further.com

Eliminating all others from this poem save yourself, man, and what it made it worse, the brutality of your reception /well we have left a misfit serenade, anachronistic whispers, slit of a wolf's eye into which to post a brazen letter // ring around that // one comprehensive guiltfear package presented via compressive anticipatory history // ring around that // and if a wood were to turn on its own trees / hurt by their individuality / and the seas rise up / in a perilous access of island envy / and our coastal regions take sides about natural processes / pitting churchmen against border guards against architects against weathering / could we make ourselves call what we have / a gift // one wanted or unwanted // I'd be first to destroy it, my bad love, without doubt

from *Blackbox Manifold*

Suilven or Humility

◇   ◇   ◇

The years idle under us as we stumble along
The ridge with our pangs and our addiction. The sleight
Of the eagle's sultry possession of air wheels
The earth round the permanence of its contour – despite
This dazzle of changelessness, still the surge
Picks up where we left off as the eagle's feather
Reaches its finale. And still the prolific urge
Grips our bodies and from unspeakable ruts
Of mind strips us and repairs our incomplete
Anatomies. This small-time act unites our
Movements as the earth without moving gluts
Itself on time. The dropping sun hauls
The millennia of each step up from sight.
The lull left in the absence of our fit
Follows through the eagle's unbroken going.

from *Poetry and Audience*

AMARJIT CHANDAN

The Prisoner Being Released

◊   ◊   ◊

Translated from the original in Punjabi by Ajmer Rodey and John Welch

One foot still in the prison yard,
he lifts the other toward a vacuum
and moves ahead like thirst
moving towards a deer.

The prisoner shakes hands with the sun
                then hugs it.
Moist-eyed they embrace.
He realises for the first time how solid
freedom is and feet and the ground.
And he starts walking on water.

from *Modern Poetry in Translation*

Swans

◇ ◇ ◇

She was brave in the bitter river,
the *Mary Rose*, doomed,
ice-chalice, lily in bloom.

Thaw, her feathers and bones dissolve in the flow
and she's gone, flower that floated
so light over death's undertow.

In lengthening light he patrols alone
ferocious on his watery shore
where the nest from last year and the year before

has drowned to a dredge of sticks and sludge.
In full sail, his body ablaze, bridge
over unfenced water, he waits for her.

The voice on the phone said,
'He doesn't know she's dead.
There is nothing to be done.'

Now love rides the river
like a king's ship, all wake and quiver,
and I can't tell him, it's over.

from *Magma*

Sandside

◊　◊　◊

Don't go: light rises up before the gull,
the fishing's good. Lower the orange line,
listen to the shallows as a crab
plays arpeggios on the mud piano,
his touch like someone picking stitches.
It's hopeless here: the tide falls,
absence stinks; no forgetting
you're coming and going. If a brick falls
it stays fallen, sparrows flit through
lobster pots and all boats shatter the sky.
A boy mimics the gulls, head flung back
gagging on air, regurgitating life
in a sound like raw sea light, its stone buds
opening, a sign of nothing but flight.

from *The Wolf*

JOHN CLEGG

Mermaids

◊　◊　◊

We'd explode from the change in pressure
before we saw daylight, and anyway
evolution has sheathed our eyes as dead ends.
We live by taste, which is really smell;
we taste what's diffused in water
and sense the direction. Carcasses mostly.

We've kept a vague idea of our shape:
wing-spindles propelling us forward,
armoured backplate, excretory organs.
But sex is a mystery. Our best guess
has males as the krill-like specks
which winkle, sometimes, under our chitin.

We sing to each other in pheromone, never
certain how message matches to sender.
Sometimes we taste our long past's echo.
We cultivate theories on the existence
of dry land, spin theologies of loneliness. We hang
translucent in love's deepwater trenches.

from *Horizon Review*

A Local Habitation

◇ ◇ ◇

Foreknowing the absence – that one day elsewhere,
Not here, oh very far from here, you will look up
And, missing something, for one split second not
Know what it is and through that heartbeat's gap
The sea will pour in that was always near

The tide of everything will break on you,
All manner of love and its own bodyweight
Of grief – foreknowing that, promise me this:
When the agent holds his hand out for the keys
And calculates the worth of emptiness

You won't unwish one thing we did but wear
Them all like beautiful impurities
In the soul's crystal and never wish we'd sat
With the wise on their dead benches on the quay
And watched our ship of fools put out to sea.

★

A man I knew, a young man back then
His childhood got him used to moving on
So he lived warily and when a good thing stopped
You'd see him close his face on it and pack
What he'd be needing next and not look back.

I will look back. I don't forget. Here I am still
Laying up the unforgettable on earth.
I learn and learn, I cannot get my fill
Of you and here and you in the here and now.
When the angels bend my dirty fingers back

They'll see the earth ingrained under every nail,
Stigmata of your nipples in each palm
And lovely harsh ghosts of your pubic mound
That so fitted. They'll contemplate a face
Glaring with all the beauties of this place.

★

To make a man not mind being over there
They should have barred him many years ago
From gardening in pleasant plots down here.
I've studied the scores of ways that things that grow
Employ against uprooting. Some thrust down

Their forks an arm's length deep, some trail
And cling on other rooted things, some cleverly snap
Leaving their living in. So many ways
Of saying I like it here. Myself with tar,
Mint, samphire, thyme and what's between her thighs

Scenting my fingers I learn better how
To get the black earth to bring good things forth
We'll like to eat next year. I'm too ingrown
In her and here to move out further than
The tide the moon drags out and lets back in again.

from *The Rialto*

An English Walk

◊ ◊ ◊

The day's a beauty, sun on the minted
morning, a fresh hint of air from the west.
The climb up Steeple track past the ox-eye
daisies, the piebald pony, the stone lintel
of the tumbled shack takes nothing from you,
nor the sheep path that veers left over rough
ground to the lip, the brow, then the crown
of the hill. Now's the time to sit and draw
in the valley's veined cupola, the next
county's border a raised vernacular
after all those flat vowels. You'd been advised
to cross an unmarked field and cut the walk
a whole arduous mile. Razor wire folds
loosely around bog grass and a haze lifts
from the soft ground. But how to do this –
slip past the way mark when you see the farmer
on the road and no convergent distance?
Now you are the girl who folds into a note
and posts herself sky-wards like a white bird.
You keep right and pass a farm where dogs
are set to guard at intervals in separate yards.
Allow now a long down hill, a rough jog
slowing as the road rises to the crossroads
and although south rolls to a village,
you follow the map and set course north
for the plantation. It's midday, water's
low, your pack an extra kilo and lunch
must wait until you've placed a wall
between yourself and the curious cattle.
The walls are man-height and you so small,
until the gate, tightly wrought barbed wire
and sheet iron layers over a nettled ditch.

She's back, the girl who can ride on air
and it's a snitch getting over this.
A cascade of tussocks on a sixty degree
slope and you've made it to the creek
where you unlace your boots and sink
your feet into the cool singing waters,
eat at last on the heat of the bank.
Lie down with the land now; you're half way back.

from *Poetry Review*

Purpose-Built Town

◊ ◊ ◊

Gradually we filled it, edged by timber frames
and rubble gardens that slowly gathered lawn.
No stones stood in the churchyard.
In the beginning, there were only children,
who skated in the cul-de-sacs, held
jam jars filled with newts to the light.
Slim Laurence sold turkeys at Christmas.
Barry had a skip business and six blonde sons,
and outside school, some of us knew,
Mrs Vanner ate cherries and sang the blues.

They chose the river Crouch:
the dry marsh where the tough grass grows,
where we crept together on our bellies;
the wet marsh known for its glossy suck
and breath of salt, the hollow wreck we dared
to clamber in. There was a boy who let his foot touch down.
The more he struggled, the more it tugged.
We watched it smooth above his head.

There's a herd of jet-black cows, printed with white numbers;
you can walk among them up to the ridge. At low tide
sheep skulls dome whitely from the brown.
One high tide neon jellies were spotted, like aliens,
under the jetty. The boys scrambled them with stones
until their lights dissolved back into river light.
If you attach a socket of meat to a string and plunge it in,
it will come up clockworked with crabs. Try it.
Drink tea from the kiosk to take the salt from your lips.

One afternoon we took scraps of bottle with us,
singeing the ants as they fled through glasswort.
At dusk the river lit up in orange streaks
while smoke rolled out along the creek.
We were allowed out of our beds and the smell
was the smell of the end of summer
and everyone gathered to watch, as the dark came down.

from *Ambit*

Failure

◊ ◊ ◊

Here is a white duck lamp, an actual
lamp, here's chips and chopsticks, no
here's my voice, a world too much, my
voice is touching the word, my hand
is touching you, when I'm listening to
you, I am, here is the George and
Dragon, then my looks flew away, I lost
them so young!, do you like my hair, do
you like my haircut, I'm toying with
an idea, of having it all chopped off,
here I'm touching the thought, of
having seen all of London, what a
pompous city, what a hypocrite,
what a fucker he never even knew
my life, here is a small girl in pigtails,
here's a life-size white duck lamp, here's
the lamp on her lap, here's a Labrador in
horn-rimmed glasses, here's a book-
shelf belonging to a wife, here's books
on the verse of submarine life, here's
books on dieting and travel, here's books
on romantic trilling, here is a children's
Encyclopaedia Britannica, my hand is
touching you, my head is touching
the syllables of your chest, here is
visibility, I am thinking, I am thinking
of trusting the ring road of London,
the M25 containing millions of pounds
of flesh like yours, and including yours,
my hand is touching the text between
us, is it a con that the body's a text
is the body flesh, I am seeing us as

ripe fruits, juicy toot, toothpaste, I
think this stage is over, I feel the
bathroom echo and this is what I feel,
come walk over to me, come and listen
to this poem, take me home write to me
write me, I feel in the consoling glassy
echoes, here in the glass, is it safe to say
love, I think, the body's just flesh, or
a thesis to poke holes in, here is this test
you keep testing me with, *test*, here is
a children's Encyclopedia Amerika, you
can prove different things with it, and my
hand is touching your hand, I am thinking
a mystery, a catflap to eternity, a glass lit
up below my feet, lit up white still I'm,
your sister, and taller in the sun, here
is the news, there is no news, or if there
was we would be it no war, a rumour
hot off the sky, and I do, I so love you
failure you will not come, probably, here
is a taxman dancing in the sun, here is
greenery, I'm sure clarity comes with
death, I'm sure poems exist, and risk
somehow hundreds of rats, and risk
somehow the roots of a tree, plugged into
whatever thought and speech is available,
here is blue craze, a mystery, I am seeing
us as a rune or truce, a floating island,
I'm desperate to assume the shape
of heroine too, here is a stick of sun
light, I must have been a trick of light, to
want it, it's true I have no point to make,
to make what I wanted, I just wanted
my clothes and my shoes, I just wanted, to
make you, I just wanted, here is you, I
just wanted, here, holding the sun light,
to here, to have you here.

from *Halfcircle*

Discontinuity

◊ ◊ ◊

I could blame da wye da sea is smoothed
da stanes; da sylk o touch; da waelin, laevin;
an will da haert be dere whin I come back?

Or I could blame da saandiloo. He wis clear
whit wye ta geng: dis wye noo, nae luikin
owre your shooder. Tide dusna wait;

see da wye da swill o joy is drained.
Dance daday. Damoarn you slip
inta eternity.

Or I could blame da hush at fills you
til you're lik ta burst wi aa da wirds
at could be said but you hadd back.

Hit's whit happens whan you step
in time, but sense a fault-line vimmerin
trowe you: dis side or dat?

Only da sea can greet an sing at da sam time:
shade an licht: cobalt, ultramarine an dan
da lönabrak – a tize, a frush o whicht.

from *The Dark Horse*

waelin: *selecting*;   saandiloo: *ringed plover*;   damoarn: *tomorrow*;   hadd: *hold*;
vimmerin: *trembling*;   greet: *cry*;   lönabrak: *surge of sea breaking on shore*;
tize: *temptation*;   frush: *splutter*;   whicht: *white*

intermission

◊   ◊   ◊

ides   glimpses of dali's eye

drawn across   producing a bird

raw and flightless

fluidity for nothing

hints of shallow pools   shackled to ice

they listened   adrift

recognising his voice

their frankish king

returns   any past fantasy fades

it would be elm   with a slight crack

saxon shield peat bogged   feeble for woden

splintered   in the hacking wall

but persevere   that boil needs attention

the metal river   pouring over

cut for soya   fossil coiling

it is the canopy we can not penetrate

there is still europe's dark forest

revelling in being revealed

where plush sheets drape around young necks

as moths dancing and mouths caressing

and with each step   he stumbles back

this darker room lit by showering light

a breeze pushed up by crashing trees

keenest blade   to cut the bull's eye

they were twins   never fighting

not for matador's sword or rag

in one final moment the cheering urged them

whitest leather bloodied

and the final film was hidden away

forward!   with lack of experience

what brews is sipped   *I had so many*

until the music began   man for man for none

at all and tilting   atlas straining

vesuvius blinking   a saxophone played

through the walls   he never catches that tune

it only emphasises the closed window

and neat sheets   outside he points

to the forest   *isn't it always as such*

in some tower   vine wrapped   ancient

there is lust   and touch and nothing else

but to find   this late autumn   dwindling.

from *10th Muse*

Damage

◊   ◊   ◊

Let me break up the lines.
          There's moonlight now.
Wet London cobbles. Shadows,
          the stink of frying onions.
Red haired, in raggy night gear,
          a merry old gentleman
offers friendship, sausages, hot gin
          to his pack of street children:
his family workshop warmer
          than the workhouse.

'My dear,' he croons, 'my dear,'
          and soon that voice is in our ears,
genius gives him life, he is loose
          in our imagination,
an 'out and outer' tapping into centuries
          of thieving peddlers.
Cruikshank gives him a woolly caftan
          cross-hatched for texture,
stands him by the fire
          with a toasting fork, like the devil.
Bill Sykes' brutality is local English.

As Fagin cowers in his cell, waiting to be
          hanged, there are some puzzles:
his name, for instance – Irish, not Ashkenazi –
          and a Bob Fagin, kind to young Charles
in the blacking factory. The choice
          is part of a writer's dream,
which has its own rules of vitality,

like the gestures of caricature;
no wakeful effort to correct the damage
by drawing Riah can begin to cure.

from *PN Review*

JANE FLETT

This Cowgirl's Lament

◊　◊　◊

A tornado and peacock were bred in his paddock;
the couple gave birth to a turquoise lasso.

It lapped round my heart, soft as oil, iridescent,
and I gave up right then on stacked shelves and school.

I fled to a ranch that was smitten with roses,
where buttercups bucked amongst horses and whips.

I learned to smoke Camels which glowed red at sunset,
a circle of fire like a solar eclipse.

My cowboy drank moonshine and kissed like a comet
his lips were chipotle, his tongue was cayenne.

He blacked both my eyes for a bet with the mountains
and locked my heart out of his opium den.

I guess he was a Mustang, his temperament feral,
he needed horizons upon which to roam.

When I scattered my Tarot it came up the Priestess,
so I bandaged my bleeding, and headed for home.

from *The Delinquent*

JOHN GALLAS

from *pacifictions*

◇ ◇ ◇

Encounter with a Taniwha near Puponga Farm, Onetahua

The deed of a Taniwha does not take time:
it is considered / done.
The doing is not to be seen.
He may put his socks on if he wishes
by thinking how nice they will look when he does.

The Taniwha lives at the westernest end of the sand
and resembles a cave at all points.
His face is a rock-face glour;
his hair abush all punga and flax;
his breath by the pulmonous salt-lac'd wave.

You are restless already with objection.
But the Taniwha is not
Nature mistook or took,
nor an eco nor logical soul.
He is Here, not About. Come on. From

his fuscous brow three chill-lit water-threads
spilled down on his tongue,
where three plastic bottles
sat like good ideas forgotten
in an empty dream of noon.

A Taniwha does not dream: and I
was sharp as August-shine
and rapt as three hours' tramp,
a nippy dawn, a glaucous beanie
and a ruck sock could be.

You are advancing tricks of light and mind:
flying saucers, mermaids,
psychic ducks, the Wurm.
But Taniwhas do not misthink,
and are not themselves a Thought.

I put up two bottles beneath two tumbles.
The third a little off.
When I turned back to behold
my stupid, slighting sport, the two . . .
stood still, half-filled, far from their taps.

You snap that currents warpled in his hair;
that fern or flax removed;
that slump and slip blah blah . . .
Ah, Nature's changelings claim the world,
but they do not move plastic bottles.

Which would be too much study to explain.
Taniwhas may do this:
why invent the truth ?
I passed the cliffs, the clouds, the farm,
and did not come to any harm.

from *PN Review*

from *Keeping the City*

◇ ◇ ◇

1 Glass

I'm moved, in cathedrals,
by how glass supports doctrine,
the joyful baptistery blaze,
saints etched in the west screen,

the allegory of nave windows
parsing the great sentence of life
as the communicant walks
back from the high altar.

But more, among ruins,
by fragments that married air
when incendiaries fell, and somehow
contrived not to melt

or be blasted to smithereens
but held fast to the promise
of endurance, transparency
which is the first doctrine of glass.

2 Cloth

Gracious Godiva shed all her clothes
to free folk from the tyranny of taxes.

Unworn, what marks a shirt as mine and no other's?
The woven name tag stitched under the collar.

All day until light went, Eve, Hilda, Keziah
worked at their looms, wore skin to the bone.

For fifty years my great-aunt sold rainbows
of silk thread from her shop on the Foleshill Road.

What takes you from rough spun to close weave?
Education, skill, learning a trade.

Cathedralled Christ in majesty
sits enthroned on his roof-high tapestry.

Through the warp of compassion
runs the woof of dissent.

3 Stone

All day I roamed the paved walkways
of pedestrian precincts,
caught my reflection
in the plate-glass windows of shops
where, a pound at a time,
I proved my existence
by an accumulation of till receipts.

Directed by fingerposts
I made my crêpe-soled way
between walls of concrete,
a pinball figure propelled
by his consumer's rapture.
I sensed my whole life surrounded
by betonised rods of steel.

Then came at last to a ruined wall
of red sandstone, centuries old, part now
of a town garden. Weeds grew
at its foot, held the stones upright
like ancient mortar. I set down
my shopping, gazed hard at the wall,
and came to myself, truly human.

from *The Warwick Review*

Wynd

◇ ◇ ◇

It's back again, the how of rain
pleating off leaky roans, binding
strands that curve down stanks, curl
by high-walled wynds and dreels,
past sweetie shops with one faint bulb,
bell faltering as the pinnied widow
shuffles through from her back room –
What can I do you for the day?
She hands me now
no Galaxy or Bounty bar
but a kind and weary face, smear
of lipstick for her public, the groove
tartan slippers wore in linoleum
from sittingroom to counter, over thirty years:
the lost fact of her existence.

Currents ravel past the draper's
where Mr Duncan and his unspeaking sister
sort shirts by collar size, set out
Mason's cuff links and next season's vests;
on stiff white cards their flowing pens
price elastic, Brylcreem, dark tartan braces.

Floods tangle, splice, uncoil
down Rodger Street, past bank and tearoom,
the dodgy garage where they sold airguns to anyone,
the steamed up window of the Royal
where fires warms the bums of silent men
who drink standing, bunnets on.
Meeting Shore Street, the river
leaps the pavement, scours a channel
through pongy weed behind the sea wall

where damp frocks shiver under umbrellas
by the market cross, waiting for their lucky day
or at least the bus to Leven
which won't come for ages, because it is Sunday.

    In the hours between *Stingray* and the evening meal,
when the strings of family, place and history
working us, are all too bleeding visible,
as gutters burst the adolescent wonders
whether to have a quick one or read French poetry.
Smouldering with solitude, the prince of boredom
stands at the window, watching rain,
wondering when life ends, or will finally begin.

    Fall, flow and ache.
By those cramped streets, the kenned wynds,
loans, closes, by-ways and dreels,
the dying shops, fishermen's damp houses
with empty sail lofts, broken pantiles,
sheds not yet ready for witty conversion;
by the constricting, cherished dreichness of our town
whose high tide had ebbed before ours began;
by the draper with its yellow blinds pulled down,
the precise angle of a streetlamp or
the budgie cage in old Jeanie's window;
by the secret path behind the wash house,
the steep slalom of Burial Brae,
the short-cuts, the chill kirks and graveyards –
by these details we did not know we loved,
we grew up provincial,
at the heart of the world.

    You are standing at the bedroom window
watching rain, homework abandoned on the desk.
The parents are somewhere unimportant,
wee brother plays keepie-uppie in the gloom -
time to belt the shorty raincoat, go
in search of nothing but the life to come.

(ii) Holly

Askew lane walked in drizzle
to Cuban boot heels echoing –
solitude marking its beat.
Sycamores drip black lopped limbs
where long-dead whalers' houses
shrug gable-ends at the sea.
In her swimsuit Stella smiles invitingly
from last night's lager can,
stoved in, out of date.
You back-heel her down a grate.
Whatever you are after, it's not that.

At the wynd-head someone leans,
unbolting the old sail-loft door.
She's been sent to put away her father's car,
a class-mate you'd sparked with at her party
though nothing more occurred, you being blate
and this East Fife, where the ancient cult
of virginity for clever girls, early pregnancy
for the rest, had two years left to run.
In those days you knew little more
than differential calculus and irregular verbs
but you knew what came next would be
definitive as Sunday in the shrouded town.
Salt in the rain on her full mouth.

★

Holly wore jeans with a man's front fly
before any lass in Fife.
She kept stapled copies of Spare Rib
below a mattress in the old sail loft.
When she'd offered them it was
far cry from girls on lager cans
with *Buy me* in their eyes.
I'd thought *patriarchy* meant the Russian Church
but through the blitz of rage and wit
I got the message that at last
not everything was down to me.
Sweet Mary, the relief!
Piled fertilizer bags against the door,

old sacks on the mezzanine floor,
in the petrol-smelling dark we got by on feel.

  Wobbly-kneed, late for my tea,
at the wynd-head I turned up
my shorty raincoat collar –
not cool but blown, thoughtless, free.
Soft in the hips, seeing everywhere
eyes blue as mussel shells,
all night there lingered
over the white noise of the sea,
a cry without words, her on my astounded fingers.

from *Edinburgh Review*

VONA GROARKE

Midsummer

◊　◊　◊

All to play for. Yesterday the rain kept hinting
it had something else to say. Today is a garden
with clothes on the line that smell of childhood
and the kind of endings that fold themselves
into tidy squares within arm's reach of the sea.
Today is tilted skylights and doors held open
with bricks. Today is next door breaking eggs
on the edge of a glass bowl. Today is a phrase
learned off by heart by asters and peonies,
by fuchsia and mallow. Also, everything between.

Tonight I will sleep on a sheet that had joy
of a bare-faced sun above the cherry tree
and tonight there will be two hundred moons
stowed between panes of double glazing
in both my dovetailed dreams of being home.

from *Poetry London*

Hart

◊ ◊ ◊

And if it was a deer that slipped between
the trees it was a thing of flesh and blood.
And if the blood was broken through the skin
it was a wound made by a lad armed with a stone
or airgun, used to prove the thing he'd seen
was real and his aim good – the stone or pellet struck
against the flank which if it wasn't gold
or rust but white as pearl or bone
was an illusion caused by moonlight
or the mist that hangs above the fields
before the sun has risen. But being
only half there and half hidden
it's as hard to pin down as any visitation;
as glancing as a moth spun
in the road at evening, or a swallow
skimming water from a river or a pool.

from *The Rialto*

Old Lad

◊   ◊   ◊

Old adam, widower of croft fold farm, nab gate,
doffs rags before the living eve of death, and laughs:
Those heaving thighs, that quickened breath
    and the enormous sighs unsettle rafter-dust
that drifts to stalls for beasts long since deceased;
He lies in laithe-loft hay-must.
    Ghost-mistress eases off his clogs.

Adust: Archaic, dry, outworn. The term survives
in written form. So may the tree be seen
depetalated by a summer storm, and later on
deleafed: A writhen thorn.
    Moss rags blow off the roof.

How paradise is lost in cowardice through married life
is daft. He waited while the oaken purlin bent
under a weight of grey stone slate until it broke.
The load was pitched into a heap. The nettles grew
and turf encroached. Unspoken for, the toppled stone
    depletes by theft without complaint.
From footings elder shoots to fruit.
    Croft fold collapse, forever incomplete.

In poetry the lines portraying impotence
must have to fail. The times on common heath or bent
with insects winging in to sting the sweated skin
within sweet hairs and sticky interstices have become
the pangs, the bites, the tunes of small–importance songs,
kept in a keepsake box of doorless keys
and unadopted coinages, as *pulchral* for
the breasts. You'd need a wrecking bar
or jemmy wrench to prise open that chest.

That's her sat here, some jenny, pulchral in the couch
just in a slip. She draws by hand her ankles in
to raise the knees and show the wrinkled rose below
her puckered nose. And that's her No, and her
          entire satire.

Old lad survives his inquisition on misogyny,
her promiscuity and gross attire, her milking plump
at pastoral stool, and in her flying rags:
          She skirts the caverns of the earth with
broom and birch, swabs steps with mop, tips slops
into the ditch. Old lad sleeps wetly with the *mollyblobs*.

Scratting naked earth for the surviving words is *poultryscrawn*.
The old lad down the risers treads the steps and so they bent.
Felt cord or worsted in the legs,
        he clogs up under edge. At stairwell springs
into his throat the lump of things gone wrong.

Old doffer lost his bobbin in the lodge.
A cloud of drizzle drifted past. Drain clogs again *disusage*.
Fungoid walls melt into heritage.

Drizzle lingers in the parlour half asleep.
        And not but what some old constructions don't
entirely disappear, but linger, as do
negatives of yesteryear, odd little tricks
        and turns of atmosphere,
as here he hung his coat up on the door,
and there the tractor sunk in alder carr.
Roofdrops tinker on some castaway enamel.
Drizzle on a field of animals. The clough nook hole
soaks damp while sun breaks out in sweat.
There drizzle drifted off: He strays his steps:
        A long wet tramp into the swamp.

The old lad frozen to a standing stone:
            His ghost is at his wake.

Come in lad, with the coal-bucket
and clanging fire-irons. Bring the scuttle to
the inner parlour. Never mind alarms.

They were clearing cloud and flying rags
by day and night. By daylight they flew kites.
The midnight saw them in the moonlight sharply antic
while it soon reclouds and things retract
            into their shadow space.

                  Hanging verse in space,
the pennants of a comico-pathetic reciprocity,

cantankerous as misfit,
inherent collapse, in rags of song.

Come in here as toast: The Poetry of Silence
in the parlour with a glass, in The Sepulchral Arms
under Barren Edge. And never mind the sirens.

from *Cambridge Literary Review*

PAUL HENRY

Usk

◊   ◊   ◊

So we've moved out of the years.
I am finally back upstream
and, but for their holiday grins
on every bookcase, the boys
were never born, it was a dream.
Here is where my past begins

in a garret beside a bridge,
woken by birds pecking moss
from the dark. The river's clear.
It will not turn to sludge
till it reaches you and the mess
of streets I hated, endured

only because you were there.
My windows are full of leaves.
There are mountains in my skylight.
Perhaps you would like it here.
It is the same river – it moves,
perhaps, towards the same light.

from *Poetry Wales*

The Elephant Whose Sturgeon-like Blood

◊   ◊   ◊

The elephant whose sturgeon-like blood
insists it was or ought to be aquatic,
whose ears, like hairy crackle-glazed chopping boards,
are cheerfully agreeing to be fans,
fingers his marulas with a trunk
strong enough to paralyse a tiger,
a trunk that's been wired up with special nerves
found nowhere else except the clitoris,
a trunk whose full time job is being free
with the slightly anarchic freedom of uncertainty;
that spends its life seeing what it's like
to live as both an arm and a nose,

a trunk that never stops embracing homelessness
even while it's guiding the elephant
past the sandy smells of sons and daughters
that smell of banks of pinks and carnations
and in and out of sand dunes and anthills
glittering with dew and small beetles
and down towards the water where the crocodiles
(that think they are unworthy, like Judas,
of being, of deserving to be, good)
are not as fast asleep as we think they are,
a trunk whose every nerve aspires to homelessness
even while it leads him safely home.

from *Poetry London*

Re-entry

◇ ◇ ◇

February 3, 2003, 8.59 EST.

It was the way the dogs behaved: circling, tracking, fanning their tails
creeping sideways, puzzled at the scent,
running up the slope then running back.
The horses stood close together and cropped the grass.

And the lake, its gentle skin was seared
now reeking under white-hot aluminium,
a mess of burning, rubber trimmed with rags
a scorched star from a logo.

Something else floated and the trucks pulled out a lump,
like a dead marlin or creature of the lake.
Hauled up, the water running off, it was ours
or part of what was ours, still smoking.
When the trucks revved hard, the horses looked up and cantered away.

Over Eastern Texas and Arkansas
at chance locations in hickory and pine
there was disturbance: a fleeing deer roasted,
jack-rabbits cooked in their holes, burnt trees, their brilliant squirrels
      too.
From the fire-towers little damage was evident-
this was smart debris.

Though much fell harmlessly in the woods,
to be discovered in future centuries on Sunday afternoons
some stuff hit the towns: hot bits spattered a glass factory;

Across the avenues, new leaves were ripped from the dogwood.
Bolts bent crazy catapulted on Route 21.
In Nagodoches someone found hair in their backyard.

A helmet was retrieved.
Grass had grown inside it, spreading where the visor was.

from *Brittle Star*

Death of Orpheus

◇　◇　◇

& since they move as a grove, the young ones, the walking ones, we regard
them as almost kin of our forest

& they shake with alternate winds, for their swaying follows an invisible sun

& we hear from the olives of Cithæron how these – yes, *women* – grow in
prolific contortions

& blow in the god's good wake to leave only pounded dust

& split fruit

& they tear at those strange, sloughable petals

& those of their fellows, till their pleached boles shine with the suppleness of
springtime

& their throats wail the wrenching of boughs, rooted terror, half-sensed fires

& at last they discover their reluctant observer; this a different *genus*

& the charcoal of his singular grief, it moves us – a still thing, a slow thing, in
the now's ever-flickering

& our high heads bow in time with the flensed lyre, wood of our wood

& too swift for our perceiving, they set to stripping his branches, husk from
seed

& a lone kernel floats down the Hebrus, in search of yielding shores

from *The White Review*

JOANNA INGHAM

The Corpse Road

◊   ◊   ◊

Six men take the corpse road to St Oswald's.
The seventh, stiff, waits on a coffin stone
as they eat their lunch, watch the sleet blossom.
The dead are heavy. Years they should have lived
pile up in them like boulders, weigh them down.
Today, the wind from the mere is grey with ice
and moss clings hard to the trees. The men drink
to the man in the box, colder than they are.

One, the youngest, pulls a lock of fleece
from the dried spikes of a teasel, thinks of
a girl he tries to please, her hair like this,
pungent and coarse in his fists. On the road,
his shoulder under his father, the boy
sees her winter eyes, her summer body.

from *Ambit*

River Dove

◊   ◊   ◊

At the school of near righteous priests
an old accordion speaks
with a deep voice of coins
and quick pain ringing
like teeth in the horse corpse.

You are among the ankles of small birds that kill.
Come, only a man with a carbide heart
could build a miracle in that blessed rock.

Halfway to glass, galvanised as
the green bottle of daybreak
in the bright world of wind and dark jute.
Intimate, thin, built with murder
in the pools and precipices of Valencia.
Wooden head, elbows of experience.
Twigs of cloth in the mouth of the river dove.

from *Brand*

ANNIE KATCHINSKA

Tawpie,

◊ ◊ ◊

the blue-eyed, the bug-eyed,
from quicksand sleep
to a stumble-and-run,
stack of bad letters swept down
to the pavement, cornflake
pie crust egg yolk slick in the hair,
on the teeth, a sock-shredded
finger drummer,
clumpy shoe,
muscle flick
and silent lip chew, lip swollen and blue,
blue shadows behind you big faces in front
just smiling,
the never-say-a-thing,
the slug tongue in p.m. light with plates and plates
of gravy 8, 8, 8
the run-up-the-street
the crossroad dash and daffodil smirk
(will get there soon will think but)
the wine-sludged, the dawn-smudged,
slow late train with a fistful of bread,
face mashed to window and silent
for quicktalk, goodtalk,
only slump and Tupperware breath
only leap-to-my feet, it's on
the other side of town will you come?
who are you my love?

from *Poetry London*

from *I, Giraffe*

◊ ◊ ◊

A Flood

I, Giraffe, 'camelopardalis',
once dappled, high on mimosa trees,
raft and dam this second flood:

they hammer feverishly beside me,
–Lilliputians with their guys and ropes–
tautening an ark against the ever rising Seine;
a dilute version of Gustave Eiffel's tower
emerges like Leviathan:
a scaffolding to save or break

my neck. Yesterday I lost sensation
in my feet but fret not for this heart
has pressure valves large enough
to lock down oceans of my blood.
'Stand proud', my father said, 'we may be lifers
in a zoo but they have made a guddle
of this damp city and all the world beyond.'

Once, he told me how we all began:
Giraffa of the order *Artiodactyla*
were trees that moved and got their spots
from strolling through the leaves
that left their shade on them.

He spoke of a creature called 'savannah',
rich in acacia and a delicious
whistling thorn; the resident oxpecker
which roamed his person like a daemon
for unwanted ticks, the black piapicks

that sieved the air for insects.

It has begun to stink. This morning
I spied a rat swim past my right hind leg.
Small fires dot the cityscape
and a man shuffles on two chairs
across the deluge. He says: 'This is a street.
There is no river here.' And drowns.
A minute iceberg crowns his debris.

Now even the gas lighters have gone
and it is dark as the bush at sunset.
Paris is a city of pontoons and floating *passerelles*
and I nap uneasily as small punts prowl
the outskirts of our zoo. At 10 I woke
to see them float the hippopotamus away,
his rump bulbous in the moonlight.
Yet he could have swum!

Ghosts of my hunted ancestors haunt my dreams:
Baringos impressed for buttons, Rothschilds
reduced to thread and guitar strings,
the bladder of a Hock stitched for a water-bag.
Parisians! I am a simple reticulated camel-cow
and abjure aristocratic forbears.
I am not good to eat! waterlogged and knobbly
I shiver as dawn floods the abandoned garden.

from *PN Review*

The Arch

◊   ◊   ◊

I have seen this arch before;
the short tunnel leading to water.
My feet were coated with dust,
that is the last thing I remember.
Just a few weeks earlier, we had
killed a goat and were celebrating
the end of the rainy season.
Suddenly, two of my cousins
took me by the legs – I thought
they were joking – and then
I became aware of the deadness
in their eyes, and was frightened.
I soon found myself underground.
The smell of soot and blood
made my nose jump around
like an ugly demon. Too many things
I cannot mention happened there.
But now I could see, nudged
by the bitter wind that blew in
from the Sahara, a very large hut
floating on water, the clothes
of a giant master hanging out to dry.

from *PN Review*

A Shrunken Head

◊   ◊   ◊

In the cargo hold,
cruising at thirty thousand feet
above blue islands,
galactically cold,
I float between Oxford and the site
where I was found

then traded on.
I cannot see for bubble-wrap.
At this stage
in my repatriation
I belong to no one, a blip,
a birdy ounce in the undercarriage.

Only the curator knows I've gone,
and who is left.
She redesigns the tour:
lizard bones
replace me, indigenous crafts
distract with dyed feathers

from an absence. So
in me no memory withstood
the leather-thonged, moth-kissed
costume of an Eskimo,
its upright hood
ringed with reindeer fur like frost,

regarding me for years
without a face
across the Victorian cabinets;
or a cruel long spear
frozen in space,
dressed like a wrist with jade and jet;

or Bobo – as I named him –
his heavy puss
pursed like a clown's,
like a freshly-sprung mushroom,
observing silence . . .
I miss being part of the known

quantifiable index,
the massive mouths of children
smearing the glass case,
sometimes shocked
and crying, more often
delighted to learn of my fate,

sneaking pictures
for school reports. Their flashes
filled me up with light
like water
would a calabash,
or cauterizing beams from night-

security did the displays.
For hours after,
I'd see patterns that couldn't be real,
shadow plays,
huge birds fighting each other
up the loaded walls;

I'd imagine
hands to rub my eyelids with,
lift them, and feel
the cross-stitches holding me in,
my vengeful breath
trapped beneath their seals,

wanting for the first
time in lifetimes to exhale,
to spit red berries
or the prattle of a curse . . .
then that would fail
in the force of my several injuries,

and I'd seem to drop
towards a far ocean,
armless, footless, a seed-head blown
without will or hope
or wishing-upon
through the middle of a crown,

to land on my shelf
under rows of wooden masks
and blown birds' eggs,
smelling the open jar of myself –
salt-sweet as tamarisk,
mild as figs.

from *London Review of Books*

Deleted Scene (The Frog)

◇ ◇ ◇

The terror lived in the shed, we knew. It was the buckled mirror
propped in the depths, in which the frog grew smaller and smaller;

poor frog, it dried up so slowly in our tin's evaporating wet –
too unthinkable to touch, too much to prod or handle, let

alone to sluice it with water. It was like a little old man –
a little old man with an old man's fingers and hands

that disturbed us to our hair-roots, while the spider on stilts of hair
stumbled over the nape of our necks and made us both shiver . . .

And I left you crouched at the door, brother, when the shed's roof-felt
so pressure-cooked the terror, and grew so hot, it'd all but melt;

I left you crouched there once I had, considering how to, stepped
through the speckled sheen of frog and mirror in one step.

The step was long, and now you're dead, I find myself wanting to ask
for some primitive forgiveness – against the slit of sky, cirrus-flashed,

you were abandoned to a space less than half a metre square
and circled yourself repeatedly, or strained into the dark from where

it was always high August and the door-slit bulged a brilliant fog
out of which you stooped and grew smaller, face to face with the frog

that looked straight through you to where more than sun bulged in;
that was just the shape of its frog-mouth, I swear it, and nothing like a grin.

from *Agenda*

FRAN LOCK

from *The Mystic and*
The Pig Thief

◊ ◊ ◊

Purple loosestrife: the runaway writes from a traveller encampment at Smithy Fen
in Cambridge.

August 18, 2003

Dear Pig Thief –

God, these English!
The sun speaks softly to them.
They walk, larded with light,
giving all things permission to grow:
proscenium dogwood, burgundy rose.
Those gardens! Those neat green fingers meting out colour!

I am in love with the English.
They do not love me back.

They love their gardens and children
and the land along the Lockspit path
barbed with stars of cow-parsley,
asterisks of damp hemp agrimony,
sour purple loosestrife.
Their love is a possessing.
They do not know the names of things
or how some plants are poison to their horses.

They are afraid of me,
say that I smell
of hot black asphalt,
cigarettes and ferrets.

They are afraid of the dogs as well.
Malkin, mongrel, all of us.

I love them anyway.
It's their gardens that make them afraid.
Their fear is a kind of chivalry.
They want to save the flowers
from cowboy tarmac, work-boots, dog shit.
They've seen how we live.

It is okay.
I am enclosing a knuckle of bud,
white with pink around the rim –
an ophry, I think, my only theft.
Please come soon and see.
It's not like home at all.

Sowing rocks: the runaway writes from a commune in Split, Croatia of the travellers' eviction from Smithy Fen.

November 11th, 2004

Dear Pig Thief –

Behind the house the continents of pine
are becoming tectonic. Soon to shift,
carry us off in a mud slide. Still no word from you.

Did I do something wrong? I worry.
Did your job fall through? Are you back
in The Aquinas Reformatory?

There were three –
hundred and eleven of them,
drove us out of Smithy.

They had meetings.
A woman said that she would like to
blow us all to kingdom come,
then let the pieces stew
in raw sewage.
The papers reported it.

Her son was in Afghanistan.

I don't like it here.
A tense light stretched between the beacon juts.
White regime of water, hammering us flat.
That puberty of cloud! Oh God!
Sky so nude and clean it makes you sick.
We unbutton our blouses and sow rocks,
seeding the sea-belly full of flints.

I don't like it here.
Bitter tea with flavoured syrup.
Occipital curve, low winter sun.
That necessary cartilage
of deadwood round the old chalk wall.
Beady, swivel-headed birds, a clutter of wing.
I will come home.

In the morning I lotus my legs.
Dust the iconostasis.
Prise apart the window.
Let the blue chlorinated daylight
sluice the bedroom.
Go over and over your lack of letter.
Someone must have told you
that I am here by now.

from *Poetry London*

Ballast Flint

◊ ◊ ◊

They often took people from these shores,
pariahs of the law or kirk. Sent them down
into the holds of ships with flint as ballast,
mined locally as plentiful useless weight.

The nodules looked like bone joints, broke
open to dark quartz, the black iris of a Sphinx,
unknowable and inscrutable. The dud cargo
was often dumped by the salt-chapped rim

of other seas where it did not naturally occur.
It's still there today, mostly, but some sparked
great fires, sharpened to double-edged blade,
a forgotten clan knapping their arms in the swash.

from *New Linear Perspectives*

Old Mutha Riah. Hoxton 1935

◊   ◊   ◊

Testing testing testing! This is Charlie
Robinson here. Are you listening Mah-rie?

I've bin trying ta get this bloody thing ta forward.
I'm doin' this on a bleedin' Chi-neese recorder.

Well, as kids we all use-ta sing 'Old Mutha Riah,
pissed on tha fire!' and being old 'nd wise now I realise

we were 'orrible to 'er, but she was a freaky little
woman, she 'ad all disfigurement in 'er face, a muzzle

like a dog, hands like paws with little claws on 'em
and all the kids use'ta say she was half-'uman,

half-'ound, although whether that was really a fact
I don't know. She was an annual attraction

at the 'Ampstead Fair! They use-ta try 'nd lift 'er skirt
up in 'Oxton market to see if she had a tail or not.

I weren't one of 'em, but she use-ta beat 'em off
with 'er walking stick 'nd if you got a cuff

round the ear 'ole you knew all about it. Anyway,
one of my jobs when I worked on the railway

was to go to Broad Street Goods Yard.
It wasn't a very nice job, as usual it was a hard

grind and the thing was it entailed terrible hours.
That day we'd bunked in round the back o'the pictures

'cos we didn't make enough money selling 'orse
manure to a bloke who took it round the 'ouses for roses.

The picture was The Weeerewolf of London with
Fredric March as the werewolf. Scared me shitless

it did 'cos I 'ad a vivid imagination, like you got Mah-rie.
So I goes to work at night but they didn't want me

so we're coming 'ome, two or three lads, out late,
'nd we 'ad to walk from a place called Norton Folgate

which was the beginnin' of Dalston High Street
and we shot right through the market,

it was all dark and dismal and miserable and rainy
and the other two lads went on their way

'nd I started down Hobbs Place, a short cut,
forgettin' Old Mutha Riah lived thereabouts.

It was a full moon that night, when the werewolf
came out and anyway, I gets just past 'er 'ouse

and 'er bleedin' windeh shot up and she poked
'er horrible face through and shrieked:

'Whassa ti-iime!? Whassa ti-iime!?'
I didn't wait to tell 'er the time! I nearly died

of fright. I rushed 'ome fast as my legs could carry
me and lucky enough your nan, Florrie,

was up and about nursing a fag and a gin
and when I told 'er she couldn't stop laughing.

from *Modern Poetry in Translation*

JAMIE McKENDRICK

King Billy's Nemesis

◊   ◊   ◊

Mouldywarp, thrower of dirt,
has tripped the horse called Sorrel
and broke the royal collarbone and killed
the King of England.

Though Jacobites toasted the little gentleman
in the black velvet waistcoat,
if push came to shove he was always
more of a Republican

and apart from a walk-on role
as the ghost of King Hamlet
till then he'd rarely shown
much passion for politics.

Three hundred years he's laid low,
airing the earth and stocking his larder
with shelf-fulls of worms,
live worms as it happens.

But today he broached the deep snow
and left one flaw in the perfect
field of white – black earth
at its core and an oval

aureole of cindery grey
with an equal mix of snow and soil.
Looks like a black wig
riding a white steed.

Now he's backed up down into the dark,
same old mole, with a bow and a scrape

or was that a wave
from his shovel-shaped mitt?

from *Poetry London*

MICHAEL McKIMM

Water Cure

◊   ◊   ◊

1.

All it takes, a simple Saturday,
Tube and DLR to Pontoon Dock,
a walk through sculpted gardens

to the sound of hydraulics, engine oil,
the Thames Barrier slowly
opening, twitchers of machinery

standing on railings,
gulls clouding and plunging,
mudlarks hoking shells, coins,

driftwood tomahawks, their long
arms beeping, their footprints
neat as ploughmen's rows.

All it takes, another watery
explore, spontaneous and strange,
side by side at the railings,

wind going at us, the river spraying
lightly on our faces – an hour or so
just standing, watching,

expecting nothing more than
turning gates, embankment noise,
gulls in competition with the wind.

2

Our first holiday abroad. The Hamway's villa
above San Antonio: cocktails by the pool,
cold tomato soup croutoned at lunch.
My old nervousness with strangers. Razor shells,
mussels, a whole cod cocooned in salt.

On the last day we got away from them,
walked before the sun was up to the nudist
beach at Punta Galera, not nude ourselves,
of course, too coy amongst the Spanish boys,
bulky Germans red as thermidor.
Underwater, snorkelling the shallow floor,
we beat through shoals of fish: yellow, red, blue.

What would I do without you? Those looks
you'd give above some teeming book,
the jokes, the G&T, your plunges into clear
warm water, the sunburn splitting our sides.
Another milestone, eh, this land without tides?

3

How long was it after we met – a week, a month –
that I showed you the exposed ten metres of Coventry's river,
spawned beneath the Burges like an open sewer?

Hardly the usual hot date stunt,
but already I knew your tastes: water
and wildlife; history's architecture.

The Sherb moved slow as estuary sludge.
Clouded flies, wire mesh, a night time crow
on the fenced verges. Kebab shop smells.

It was not love, then, not yet.
It was the joy in finding someone
who would watch a slowing river for an hour.

How much later after that, pacing home
through a Ring Road underpass,
did I stop and ask, 'Would *you* marry *me*?',

knowing how you'd feel, knowing
that a law would soon be passed to make it real.

4.

I think of you that day we 'Causewayed'
and it was more than I could have imagined.

You stood on the furthest sea-weeded stones,
far beyond the Mackintoshed tourists,

gales on your back, your fringe clinging wet
beneath the hood of your coat, your smile

wide at the danger: huge anxious waves
rising and falling and almost never crashing,

just swelling a foot above head height, black
and torrential, tempting to rupture the rocks.

And I know I did not take your hand.
To pull you back or go down under with you –

I could not take it. But they'd have known it all
from my yelling voice: joyous, spray-stung, yelling.

from *The Warwick Review*

HUGH McMILLAN

Too Big a Part

◊ ◊ ◊

Last night the girls got their parts in the nativity.
Lydia is reprising last season's triumph as the
Angel of Glory, all blondeness and glitter
looming like a valkyrie over star-struck shepherds.
Jasmine is to be Mary and distraught
to be pushed into the big time so soon.
We try to reassure her. Mary is the easiest,
we say, she doesn't speak, all she does is follow Joseph
and stand around with a baby. There's sheep, we say,
and you get to ride the donkey, but to no avail.
Jasmine stands at the window, tears mirrored
in the fat glass, as unsure of her place in the very centre
of the puzzle as presumably that woman then, turning
in her palm over and over, the luck of the world.

from *The Rialto*

What Will Happen To The Neighbours When The Earth Floods?

◊   ◊   ◊

Sometimes I mistake Noah for God, but sometimes I mistake God for no one.

I mistake Noah for God because even in his arms I'm abandoned.

From my High Ground you can see my neighbours, but it's hard to look.

So here are my glasses.

Is that a raft? Because I think it's a boatman who hangs his head in the storm.

But is that a raft or is it a rock? Could it be one rock lower than Ararat?

I love my neighbours and I think God would love me for this.

But I covet my neighbours too, and God might proscribe this if he had laws.

Look at my neighbours with nothing to covet. Now see the container I live in with too much to hold.

There are my neighbours; here's my container.

Here's me, the doves, the griffins, the dogs, the bears, the boys, and my man who can look like God when the weather's not clear.

And the weather is unclear a lot.

I remind him of the neighbours, but he says, 'Look. I don't want to be reminded of the neighbours.'

I can be distant with him, but I feel affection when he eats.

When he eats, he bows his head like that boatman who probably isn't a boatman but a neighbour pressing against the weather on almost the last land in the world.

from *New Welsh Review*

Bob's Dogs

◊ ◊ ◊

There was the one dog, neither use nor ornament.
Each morning he lurked by the tanker's dribbling spout
licking his chops. Spawned every cur in the district.
Bit the postman, once, and got away with it.

There was the other dog, two-bit brother to the first,
eyes like spilt milk. Danced on the slurry pit's crust
one time to many, said Bob, and no good since.
Bit the builder's foreman twice, and got away with it.

There was the third dog, each month went walkabout
under a chicken moon, fetching and shedding stars.
Deaf to everyone but Bob's dad, now four years
bed-bound. What shall I say? Bit nobody, yet.

And lastly there was the bitch. Bit the child.
The four shots blew through the lanes and echoed loud
in the neighbour's eyes. Only Bob shook my hand,
hitching his trousers up with a 'Welcome, my friend'.

from *New Welsh Review*

Bog Bodies

◇ ◇ ◇

I

Outside you all grow older,
Have a change of heart, move house in the summer.
But underneath, faces build on centuries of lost teeth
Canine, wisdom, raw molars, rotting
Jaws crisscrossing like jackdaws in woods.

Lost count of how long we've been here.
Can't tell a daybreak from a duskfall.
All I know is that I love you, enough
To deepfreeze, to rust, to plug my ears with dust.

Wrapped up in bedcovers of earthy water,
We dream the mud of the bog, the dud of the wetlands
In our blood, drowning in dirt, untouched, undug.

Somehow the animals don't find us; can't claw what's left
With fake nails and blindness. Can't even smell us.

We survive under the landscape. Dog-flesh, skeletons gone
But still there somehow underneath the peated eiderdown
Of the dead years when we don't speak.

Repeatedly pulling earth over our shoulders
We are neither water nor land, storm or stillness,
Like fishes that sleepwalk on mountains, horses that don't drown.

In a dampbed we wait between realms.

II

Winter came like a cough caught in chests.
The ground froze around us.
Wheezy, breathless, still becoming bog, we half-lived,
Half-forgot. A rib-cage here and there.
A front tooth. Not a lot.

Not everything I touch is lasting.
Not even bogland,
Not even men.

He got up and walked away washing his clothes,
Scooping the dirt from his eyes, unsheathing himself from
Bogteeth like a wet dog after rain.

Only I remained. A set of eyelids sewn shut. Dreaming of mudsling,
The land being torn up.

III

Spring. We are scalped heads. Lonely bodies,
Separately skulled.
I couldn't pull myself up behind him. Disturb the sewage of trees.
The flood of quietness around me.

So you all grow older without me,
Have a change of heart, move house in the summer,
Leave me to imagine in the dark.

Hip bones, kneecaps, thighs,
Outgrown body parts,

What's left is enough, you can rub it between finger and thumb,
It takes time to shrink wounds. To dry blood.
To knock seasons from the soles of your feet.

I let the bog hold me until I'm ready.

from *Clinic*

KIM MOORE

The Drowned Fields

◇　◇　◇

Although being without him now
would be like standing on one leg
still everything seems paper thin.

If my foot slips and breaks the surface,
I'll fall to a land of drowned fields,
where the only language is the language

of the sky and the birds make endless
patterns in the air and the pools of water
are words the rain has left behind.

Next to the path the grass moves beneath
my feet. Hummocks store black water
while his thoughts, impossible to ignore

push their way across the land like large
enthusiastic dogs. The lives I could
have led are silver threads across

the drowning land and birds come
together, then spread apart, as if the sky
opened its hand and let them loose.

from *Clinic*

Ballad of the Moon, Moon

◊ ◊ ◊

El aire la vela, vela.
El aire la está velando.

after Lorca

A pettelengra boy whacks petalos on his anvil.
  The moon slides into his smithy, bright as a borì.
The boy can not stop himself staring. The moon
  releases her arms in flames of flamenco,
her sweet dress slipping from one shoulder.
  'Nash nash, choon, nash nash, choon, choon.
If the Rom catches you he will splice your zi
  He will smelt your soul for miriklè and vongustrì.'
The moon smiles, 'Chavvo, let me kur my kellipen.
  By the cherris the gyppos come, they will find you
poggadi on the anvil with your biddi yokkers lelled'.
  'Nash nash, choon, nash nash, choon, choon
Run for it, moon, run away, moon, fair moon.
  I can hear the hooves of my horse masters hammering.'

'Chavvo, muk me be. Don't pirro upon my pawni
  ringi so rinkana'. The drumskin of the plains thrums
with hoof-strokes. The boy backs across the smithy.
  Horse masters hove through the night-tree
a forest in slow motion, bronze and dream.
  Bronze and dream are the Roma their eyes sky-high,
their gaze lances through walls of world and smithy.
  But the moon dances her prey to the snare of a mirror.
She hauls the pettelengra o kolè dyoonaste to the pliashka.
  The gypsies ride at her trailing veils, her mokkadi doovàki.

The wind whips by, wraps the moon in her purlènta.
It wraps that bride, the moon, the moon, *barval, bevvali!*

from *Modern Poetry in Translation*

Romani: **pettelengra**: blacksmith; **petalos**: horseshoes; **borì:** bride; **nash**: run away!; **choon**: moon; **Rom**: Romanies; **zi**: heart, souk; **miriklè**: necklaces; **vongustrì**: rings; **Chavvo**: boy; **kur my kellipen**: do my dancing; **cherris**: time; **poggadi**; broken; **biddi**: tiny; **yokkers**: eyes; **lelled**: locked up; **muk**: let/allow; **pirro**: tread; **pawni**: whiteness; **ringi**: dressed; **rinkana**: spruce; **o kolè dyoonaste**: beyond, in the other world; **pliashka**: Romani ceremony before wedding; **purlènta**: silk headkerchief; **mokkadi**: dirty; **doovàki**: veil; **barval, bevvali**: wind.

Passed

◊ ◊ ◊

The dead are with us; amongst us
    I mean. You can tell them by the
cold tips of their ears, the yellow
    flames that issue from their lips
instead of speech, the odd way you
    still know what they mean, each one
leading us somewhere important, to
    a crime scene or some other kind
of slaughter – war or marriage.
    They walk slowly, stately, as if bearing
the weight of lilies; they pass right
    through each other and don't seem
to care, their pockets full of bright
    untarnished change or spangles
of frost. They spend their days lost
    somewhere we don't know or ever
mention; at night they throng our
    dreams under snow-tipped trees in
empty city squares that seem Eastern
    European with stray trams brightly
lit like a set right out of a spy film
    where others are always watching
from high buildings in unfurnished
    rooms. They're not unfriendly, the
dead, in their involuntary way; they
    don't mind much if we borrow their
stories or memories or ignore them
    or even reach to touch. I find your
hand to translate from sleep instead
    count your fingers like a newborn
watch the curtains breathe, rehearse
    an introductory phrase I'm everlastingly

too shy to speak, seeing them turn
       from me then disappear through their
smiles like sunset through last drinks
       or rainbows oiling the river's quay.

from *The Rialto*

Free style

◊　◊　◊

I come home from work on the second day back.
The word *value* has been on everyone's lips,
while the month has been saying goodbye
to heat and blue skies with blue skies and heat.
There's a message on the phone, and so I drop my books,
hurry down to the field where the picnic, half-eaten,
is spilt over the rug, and the cold bags lie open and where
the river has cut through the sandstone's gold rust,
and sheep's hooves have made small mountain passes,
winding down the steep banks. Down in the water where
my friend is swimming, the sand clouds behind her.
Her daughter is swimming too. And the dog is swimming,
a wet dab of black under the willow's floating wool.
It is September's last day for wild swimming,
the gnats and flies treading air over mud and dung.
My friend's daughter, who is also my friend, has come
home to us. She has come back. Her long hair streams in the water,
going with the flow of the river's weed. And I think how swimming
is like reading, or surviving, and how it's possible to slip back
into the river's writing, into the current's flow, and how,
when the weeds backstroke through the water,
they look up through the alders and willows to the sky,
become green rippling lines, intuitive, inevitable
as you hope the lingering trout will be.

from *The Poet's Calendar*

Sardines

◊   ◊   ◊

After the yard was cleared, where could he hide?
I looked behind the haybarn, in the old screen
where the pines had grown too gaunt
to hide anyone. I looked in the stall
which still held some of the smell of hay
and harness, but he wasn't there.
I looked of course in the obvious places:

in the chapel, where he might have ended up,
eating grapes in the confession-box,
or behind the high altar where you stood
on tiptoe to get the hooded candle-snuffer
to reach the flame. But still no sign.
Maybe he'd stopped playing, sick of all the times
you'd called out 'It isn't fair! I don't know

the rules for where you can hide and where not.'
Maybe he was back in his own place,
above the mountain or beneath the sea,
where it was no longer possible
to creep in beside him, hardly daring
to breathe, waiting for the voices of the others
to fade in the distance, well off the scent.

from *13 Pages*

Immigrant Song

◊   ◊   ◊

mutual intelligibility – lonely time
weather wise roused
mine measured by a foreign model

frændr inhospitably near their own
throstle song hush – said grief
far inland from breakers dark frame

come to name wave upon shore
as before – light that lingers
still in the state of a whelping birth

tell me friend what ruin gives out
incongruent but salient worth
rushing with such shudder from seas

from *Poetry Wales*

RUTH PADEL

Ripples on New Grass

◊ ◊ ◊

When all this is over, said the princess,
this bothersome growing up, I'll live with wild horses.
I want to race tumbleweed blowing down a canyon
in Wyoming, dip my muzzle in a mountain tarn.

I intend to learn the trails of Ishmael and Astarte
beyond blue ridges where no one can get me,
find a bird with a pearl inside, heavy as ten copper coins,
track the luminous red wind that brings thunder
and go where ripples on new grass shimmer
in a hidden valley only I shall know.

I want to see autumn swarms of Monarch butterflies,
saffron, primrose, honey-brown, blur sapphire skies
on their way to the Gulf: a gold skein
over the face of Ocean, calling all migrants home.

from *The London Review of Books*
collected in *The Mara Crossing* (Chatto & Windus)

Pomegranate

◇   ◇   ◇

The soldier boys know nothing
of the world but how to end it;
nothing of books but how they burn.
Fire's another slow reader
to begin with, then it skims,
remembering all it knows already.

Today the town square's primordial
with mist and smoke, a smeared
flask of new beginnings; flames
well into their stride are strenuous
with cartloads of the mint and foxed
guilty of being on the wrong shelves.

And last of these, the luscious herbals.
Speed-edited for wormholes
and disinformation, they split, spill
their tinted cornucopias; fruit rises
blazing and exotic then descends
to seed the square with purer black.

Better than scandal sheets or almanacs,
agreed, but maybe we've seen endings
enough where nothing grows but hunger;
and soldiers with their sooty bayonets,
they're known to get bored with embers,
to remember other work they have.

So fades the evening's entertainment.
Pinched streets begin to fill the way
leaves and ashes clog the fountain
where the daft woman will spend her night,

begging for any fruit to spare, begging
the soldiers for her daughter back.

from *Stand*

An unborn child wonders if it's worth it

◊　◊　◊

They say the seas catfight by night,
that rabbling gales scorch huddled girls?
Well, toffee, Haiti howls, that's right.

Lizards and ladies stoned in deserts,
rows of heads popped by rocks in red little shocks?
Oh, poppet, the tongue that cocks will cop it.

And grannies and mice are vial mummies in cold countries,
mummies in others suck gun through their gums?
The choice, Lucy Locket, is yours to grace this earth.

Liver, cornea, lymph rotted from rust in water,
babies burping the expiration of suicide daddies?
Every little helps through WaterAid monthly, kiddo.

But the tremor of stars stirs furious lovers together?
Yes. Points and counterpoints horrify me.

And the migratory Brahminy kites swoon at Lake Chilika?
Pumpkin, most folk are wanting to flee.

Maybe I'll whistle to see who picks up my tune?
Weigh it up, petal, maybe we'll see you soon.

from *Magma*

Sole

◇   ◇   ◇

we shift the tables so that
wood grain faces boats beached
in silt and Midday fog thick as bisque. They
come, two by two, thoughts in their
pockets, summer shirts limp with sea air. The afternoon is
yellow as a two-day-old bruise, an aftertaste
of rhubarb and pastry cream. The minutes crumble
like salt flakes, like fish flesh in the grating. The minutes
are brushed crumbs, looped smears of water trimmed
with crumpled white linen. Two by two they come,
they go. They carry in them all the minutes broken
into pieces, drunk down with sparkling water, sparkling
disappointment in their Sunday beer.

from *The Delinquent*

PASCALE PETIT

Notre Dame Father

◊ ◊ ◊

Under the Seine I burrow,
through the medieval cellars of Paris,
from the Rue de la Huchette to Notre Dame.
Swimmer of sewers,
rat-father of jazz caverns and oubliettes,
haunter of nightclubs and dungeon vaults,
trapdoor and manhole opener,
dancer of the catacombs.
I am the father who searches beneath the water
and above the air, flying father,
ascender of four hundred steps
to the North and South Towers.
Father of the Chimera Gallery,
my names are Howler, Gnawer, Goat.
Eroded father, I lightning out.
I am the angel of the great nave roof
blowing my bugle.
Throat father, I gurgle forth.
I am a dove perched on a demon,
my beak always open.
My heart is a rose window.
Quarry father, stroller of the necropolis,
caretaker of the Quai St Michel,
resident of Les Argonautes hotel,
my gargoyle eyes see the insides of things.
I am the gypsum and limestone father,
my left foot is a crypt
and my right a foundling hospital.
Doctor and priest father,
who heals as he wounds,

I go in and out of the realm of death
to where the sicknesses crouch.

from *Magma*

JACOB POLLEY

Lunarian

◇ ◇ ◇

There's a man in you, his face like melted tallow,
for yours are the old words and yours the old
unusable, soot-grimed things. I spy you tonight,
one night from full, through a pair of cheap binoculars,
hauling up the mountainside your gong of chalk.
If there were a pond nearby upon whose surface
you might lean your subtle silver highness,
I would try to gaff and grapple you, out of courtesy,
for some nights there's more bulge to the seas,
more reflectance from your coal-bright craterscape.
But tonight unreason separates from reason,
as oil from water, dark from light, bedspread
from blackout cloth, your reflection from yourself,
O creamy, scraped-out shell of a king crab caught
off a north-east sea-coal beach, no less a beach
for glittering black, its anthracitic curve laid down
along the length of my occluded early mind
at grandpa's house in Newbiggin where I heard
at night the harbour bell clonking like a bell
around a black goat's neck. O caprine sea! O grandpa dark!
There's a moonlight man with cords of silk who binds
the destined together, but tonight my mind's
undone, great turner-away, O whole of holes,
walnut of night! You turn the tides, so give me blisters,
burn my retinas, break my heart; prove by silence
that the mouth that speaks the moon should whisper.

The night is still. The stars are fixed.
You are the moon, your silver dress,
your disappearing constancy.
The night is still. The stars are fixed:
we move through phases of the flesh.

from *13 Pages*

After

◇   ◇   ◇

After the families picnicking beneath the trees
on spread blankets among bluebells and wild garlic,
women unpacking baskets, cutlery chiming

while men lean back on their elbows and children
compete in a maze of grass stems
for the dandelion with the longest stalk –

after the boys shinning up a solitary conifer,
clustering in its darkness like excited birds
and sending down a shower of needles

while their older siblings sprawl on the benches
smoking and studying their mobiles
and a pair of lovers lie in each others' arms

and a lone girl reads in the centre of a meadow
for an hour without moving as an impromptu
football match plays out around her –

after the clamour, the running and laughter,
the park alight as a weekend beach
flooded by the April sunshine into colour

he comes the next morning, early, bent over
in his pale coat, with his long spiked pole
moving slowly, carefully along paths and borders;

before light has touched the lowlands of Flanders
or the belfries pinned to the horizon
he appears like the mist itself compacting,

spearing all remnants, sweeping the ground clean,
grass closing again behind him,
nothing to say where anyone has been –

he comes like an owl at dawn, eerie, half there;
he comes the next day as surely as the day itself
and the one after that, and the one after.

from *The North*

ANNE ROUSE

High Wall

◊ ◊ ◊

Behind a bricked-in yard you could hear the alley
where lorries backed in, to the kvetching of a drill.
Damp ivy grew over the wall, and I set out marigolds,
little suns against the grime, and forgot to replace them when they died.

Nothing ever went wrong – the noises thinned, enfolded;
the window stuck shut, the bricks aged, worn and high –
but in time I climbed out, into nothing's weeds and blight,
and felt what was hidden: a tearing anger at the living, and found

a gash in the earth, a fallow groove, and turned up the ground,
to bring on the dry, flecked seeds of grass –
the blazoning tint of which could be seen, newly insistent,
in the loam this morning: an undulant, unyielding green,
when I crouched down and looked, with you, and the child.

from *Poetry Review*

Experience

◊   ◊   ◊

The widow will weep for her beau, my dear
While the spring grass continues to grow, my dear

Life's lengthy or short but it ends when it ends
We arrive and we go and that's so, my dear.

The elected must govern, the masses must vote
Every man has his price (*quid pro quo*, my dear)

But God seldom bargains and never in Lent
For he's too busy fighting the foe, my dear.

The moon eats her heart out again and again
Though the rivers just go with the flow, my dear

An earth worm divides well, a country does not
And sometimes a yes becomes no, my dear.

Our wishes all fall down the well with a splash
There are decades of echoes but oh, my dear

Give up what is lost if you can't fish it back
Just keep walking. And that's all I know, my dear.

from *Poetry Review*

ZOË SKOULDING

The Man in the Moone

◊ ◊ ◊

it's always night before the words and in this
silence something startles out of nowhere
crashes into earth with no one to look back

or say what a body was before and what has
changed in it as fingernails crescent into moons
to shadow month by turning month

or what is the name of this silence all steely
reflection still waning where the moon
slips away under cover of detectable traces

what it looks like from here is all I can tell you
now it's all push and pull all yes no maybe
all credit and loss all of it passing through

the others I am speaking I am walking I am
eating I am sleeping I am writing only I
could have written this only you will read it

★

the future was invented with its tense
a shadow falling where our atmospheres are
breath on windows sun scoring lines into skin

a sentence reverses itself between two
pairs of eyes discovering a distance suddenly
exposed in words that run on without stopping

for you to be anything without them
the timbre of the body half sound half

weight as if between us thought were pressure

distributed in music the tension of a
single note everywhere between breaths
holding inside it weight and distance in

gravity as tightrope stutter they row
themselves through air with giant fans and
utter their minds by tunes without words

★

since the impact event you've carried
strange dust in your throat farther and
farther away the saying and not

being able to the being and saying and not
knowing how to at the limits of a tongue
lost in orbit circling and circling

and burning up starry Laika out there
somewhere as dog dust cold wars racing
through the politics of dream space

it is exactly this far and no further
the moon eclipsed by the idea of moon
cut out and leaning through the night

a blue that eats away at stones the sky
heavy with it in the distance drifted by a
word shaken loose from border controls

from *PN Review*

wulfmonath

◇ ◇ ◇

this scowl is nothing more than
winter burn
      blood lines,
       scorched + spun.   thread
+ weave / thread + weave this
woven   thread

Aa see you. akin to speculation
forward   aye
                    aye
               aye
           here's the cusp

first born. all knowing
bak + forth bak + forth
ice bound . heart of oak . leden

yuz think me aad-farant,
wading through the human
swirl mute as shadow.
I do.   I done.

S L A I N   By the A66 Pagan
Wanderer Lu fixed me in Vinyl
and I not hardly wry wit fingers
hup/stick frozen, frequently I,
instead pretend to like mittens
being fond + stupit + tired of
me life.

Dear Skald, I amm certain you
know of Leaf Cutter John +
Johnny me Laddie + Johnny in
the Poke. We are Border
Reivers; breeding quickly +
prolific like, living + feeding on
garbage + faeces like, Musca
domestica with shiny
new hands.

Swine Forkbeard has become
King of Denmark.

You think its clivver. I wish I
could tell ah I luv ah + it not be
too soon. She is smaller +
slender, no sharp upward
bent + cheeks still rosy with
choke-damp. Do I tekk yr fancy
with me hare-lip + hirple?

Swine. Two hours to go and
still your resolve is not weak
en/ in

I kick me self, for I have missed
Leaf Cutter John + now,
Forkbeard, the swine with
spines + bristles + not tekkin
none of yr nonsense [how]
obliterates owt that gets in the
way. Wuhd best make refuge
of the midden.

from *Cambridge Literary Review*

ANNE STEVENSON

It's astonishing

◇   ◇   ◇

that this is my wild left foot I'm freeing from a Lycra sock,
that these arthritic fingers once belonged to my bow hand,
slaves to a cello named Caesar and to Johann Sebastian Bach
whose solo suite Number 5 in C minor, the Sarabande,
is quietly fingering my memory: resignation and truth.
That I can lean over, flick a switch and a light will go on
surprises me, as does nodding to sleep, book in hand, and flicking it off
to revive in the dark a young cello-playing Anne Stevenson
along with strict Mr Troostewick (Troosey) in New Haven
and soft-spoken Mr Edel, feared and adored in Ann Arbor;
both by now dead, still living in their beautiful instruments. Even
Herr Haydn, Signor Boccherini, M Saint Saens and Mr Elgar,
long dead, are alive in those concertos I never quite learned to play
before I listened to my deafness. This is my left foot, poetry.

from *Poetry Review*

The Curtain

◇　◇　◇

Perhaps you know that story where people
step out of this world and into another
through a particular split in the air;

they feel for it as you would your way across
a stage curtain, plucking at the pleats,
trying for the folded-in opening through which

you shiver and shoulder yourself
without a single acknowledging glance up
to the gods, so keen are you to get back

to where you were before you made your entrance:
those dim familiar wings, you invisible,
bumping into things you half-remember

(blinded as you'd been out there
in the onslaught of lights, yes, blinded
but wholly attended to in your blindness).

Imagine our dying being like that,
a kind of humble, eager, sorrowless return
to a place we'd long, and not till now, known.

No tears then. Just one of us to hold
aside the curtain – *here we are, there you go* –
before letting it slump majestically back

to that oddly satisfying inch above the boards
in which we glimpse a shadowy shuffling dark.
And when the lights come on and we turn to each other

who's to say they won't already be
in their dressing room, peeling off the layers,
wiping away that face we have loved,

unbecoming themselves to step out
into the pull and stream of the night crowds.

from *Poetry London*

CLAIRE TRÉVIEN

Sing Bird

◇　◇　◇

Vile   Birds fried to the wires – electric funambulism
Violins   played by the jaded weaves of a rainstorm
Violins steal   sautéed voices trapped by melted claws
Violin-stealth   – the surprising street-corner orchestra
Violins steal the vows   of a shackled bandstand of brothers
Violins steal the voices   that have lost the page and wing it
Violins steal the voices-off   with some gin-soaked inspiration
Violins steal the voices of whim but I've seen how their jaws open
Violins steal the voices of women under stress
'Violins steal the voices of we men too'   mechanically
Violins steal the voices of women to put in there   as if they had fried in their
Violins steal the voices of women to put in their   cage of shoulders and hip

from *Fuselit*

The Life Cycle of the Fly

◊   ◊   ◊

The housefly on the ceiling,
his maggot does the thinking.
His maggot is the undried fly,

the dreamy fly that lives inside
the black and brittle crate,
and is its creamy pilot.

He swells himself on levers
to make the wings buzz,
to make the legs go,

to move the rough eyes about,
to send out the long lips,
and make himself seen by that

pappy grub of the other sex,
who's loose inside her derelict,
washed-up box of blackened wood;

though the glint of her, a glimpse
of her white give is given
through the timber's winking split.

Before she was boxed
and grey ribbon-bowed with wings,
the maiden maggot writhed

as though she was in pain
and fit to pop. She seemed to mean
to throw her own self off herself,

or to take issue with her own will,
or to find the very air disgusting,
but au contraire, she was laughing

and her entire body was her smile,
her smile being all teeth,
her segments each a tooth.

I loved you as that maggot
that you were, and licked,
you shone like one.

You were not yet the fly
you would become,
the mourning-black contraption

which arises on the other side
of the pupa's brown casket
to carry off the cargo

of her doughy soul.
How bleak she looks, the fly,
uncovered as she is by gloss,

ensconcing as she does
all the burnished lacquer
of her worm.

from *Poetry London*

Marstrand

◊　◊　◊

The juts of island with a fortress where
Sweden tried out solitary confinement
for five cold years, and one victim went strange
and chiselled his fingers to putrid stumps
in the window stone.

               A great cormorant
on a boulder, staring through itself
at fleeting, darting shoals of silver-black,
stirs, slaps the inlet to shudders
and rises in steady flight.

from *Stand*

Delft

◇　◇　◇

I promise when I pack up the clogs,
raise them to chime with one chipped toe
your passing; when I glue back a pleat
in the skirt of the lady with pale blue hair
whose apron said *B ugge* after she fell
down the stairwell revealing a bell
beneath her dress on which a windmill
was waving goodbye to four birds
reflected in the inky water; when I wrap
the cold tile where your butter flattened
the sheaves of hay combed to a tuft
in the still wind in which etched-in cows
stared out under low clouds looming over
a walled garden whose gate I longed to
walk through always – I promise the glaze
will be wet on all your Delft, on both my hands.

from *Magma*

Questions about the Demon Taotie

◇ ◇ ◇

Translated from Chinese by Pascale Petit

The Pole Star is set in the centre of his forehead.
The deep blue   is crystalline   his ice pupil
has destroyed everything   Does the lonely
boiled girl embrace everything?

Escaping from Anyang   is an escape into the Yin night
No other light except this sight
luxuriously grinding a huge axe
Where did the tender broken limbs fall?

Looking up   for thousands of years
we sink down   Water always grinds its teeth
beneath us   the girl collapsing to a gurgle
Does Taotie seize   or chew?

Thousands of words re-split open are still
the one character   that one stroke captures life's flow
has been cooked ten thousand times   the flesh still soaked in sorrow
to reawaken   Is seizing   chewing?

This face is even more ruthless
than non-being   this powerlessness
staring out rams a hole
to pound away   What beauty is not bloody?

Our floating life is carved
on the shallow bronze relief   Does

the pupil's axle icily shrink space?
How many suns don't rise or set in the darkness of naming?

The girl swings gracefully back from the Yin
night   Does a thin fragrance snuff out all light?
Do bestial and human faces gently clasp vapour?
Has unutterable language   finally fulfilled the sacrifice?

from *Poetry Review*

The Birds

◊ ◊ ◊

They pack up around three with their incessant chirping.
Their headgear includes goggles, stripes, crests, and masks.
They peck for a living for their grub, which sometimes includes grubs.
They snack on gingerbread and candy corn from off witches' houses.

On the ground they look helpless. Their hopping looks absurd.
Their tiny brains contain thoughts about worms; fluff; other birds; and goats.
(What kind of weird-ass animal has a beard but can be milked?)
They switch into defensive mode whenever a goat or person comes round.

Their brains are so small they forget how to fly until they do it.
If you make them cross, they'll poop on you.
If they see a witch they chirp, 'Witch!' and retreat to a safe distance.
(The witches want to bake them and use their feet for coathooks.)

Their nests may be built out of yarn and dental floss.
They keep spare nuts in select locales for future munches.
They pick on smaller birds to practise seeing off predators (like the witches).
They keep their eggs hidden under bushes, like jellybeans or spiders.

If you cross them, they'll pluck your eyes out.
Their heads are the same size as dolls', but their bodies won't fit in the clothes.
If they spy a goat they try to confuse it by flying backwards in slow-motion.
They want to live on the ground like people, but they can't be arsed to make
    weapons.

from *PN Review*

CONTRIBUTORS' NOTES AND COMMENTS

FLEUR ADCOCK was born in New Zealand but has lived in England since 1963. Her collections of poetry, all published by Bloodaxe, are: *Poems 1960–2000* (2000) and *Dragon Talk* (2010); a new book, *Glass Wings,* is due in 2013. She has also published translations from Romanian and medieval Latin poetry, and edited several anthologies, including *The Faber Book of 20th Century Women's Poetry.* In 2006 she was awarded the Queen's Gold Medal for Poetry. She writes of 'Bees' Nest', 'This poem is one of a series about my encounters with insects and other arthropods. All the details are true – it is a matter-of-fact description of what seems like a piece of magic. The bumblebee is a particularly welcome visitor, and to find one building in long grass at the edge of my lawn struck me as an honour. On a previous occasion when a queen bee attempted a nest in my garden it failed, which made the success of this one even more exciting. I spent hours watching the worker bees disappearing into the grass and later emerging mysteriously from underground. The timing was perfect, too: it happened to be a summer when two of my granddaughters were visiting from New Zealand, with their parents, and I was pleased that the girls shared my fascination with the cute creatures.

'As the mound of cells began to expand upwards the bees carried tiny strands of dried moss to camouflage the roof; I couldn't help seeing it as a skull erupting very slowly from below, and was delighted when the image of the Green Man occurred to me. I also found the subject gave scope for having some fun with 'buzzy' sound effects. The poem ends with a dying fall, as do several of those I wrote about insects, because of the depressing decline in their numbers. If bees die out we're all in trouble, and bumblebees, with their admirably independent ways, tend to be misunderstood, unlike the much cultivated honeybee. People confuse them with wasps, and imagine that they'll sting, which they practically never do. They are altogether good news.'

PATIENCE AGBABI was nominated one of the UK's Next Generation poets in 2004. She is celebrated for the live performances of her poetry. She has lectured in Creative Writing at several UK universities including Cardiff and Kent, and is currently a Fellow in Creative Writing at Oxford Brookes University. Agbabi has published three poetry collections, the latest being *Bloodshot Monochrome* (Canongate, 2008). She is currently completing a contemporary version of The Canterbury Tales for which she received a Grant for the Arts. She is blogging the creative process at patienceagbabi@wordpress.com

She comments, 'This poem is a version of "The Tale of Melibee", from The Canterbury Tales. The original begins with a promising dramatic incident – Melibee's wife and daughter have been attacked – and is followed by twenty pages of dry debate between Melibee and his wife on what actions to take against his enemies. The tale is also in prose, and, unlike most of Chaucer's work, not linguistically inspiring. I decided to highlight the moral dilemma facing the hero and as I'm a film noir aficionado, it reminded me of the genre's exploration of the grey areas of the human psyche. In noir, setting is of prime importance. My setting is Gravesend, the same setting the BBC used for their Asian noir version of "The Shipman's Tale"; it's also the setting for *The Long Memory*, a British noir starring John Mills. I desperately wanted to base some of the action by the river and this gave me the idea of using the specular form. I had used the form once before and was confident that the content would fit. The device of unreliable narrator has always interested me. I started jotting down phrases and lines that would read both ways. My initial idea peaked with the hero gazing into the river at his own reflection, a concept I've since used for another poem. The quotation came later and was serendipitous: I'd watched and admired Christopher Nolan's film *Memento*, a neo-noir with the entire narrative enacted in reverse. I read his brother's short story on which the film was based, and the quote perfectly emphasised my central themes.'

TARA BERGIN is currently studying at Newcastle University for a PhD on Ted Hughes's translations of János Pilinszky. Her poems have been published in *Poetry London*, *Poetry Review*, *Modern Poetry in Translation* and *PN Review*. A selection of her work appears in Carcanet's *New Poetries V*. She writes, 'It was during my PhD research into Ted Hughes's translations of the Hungarian poet János Pilinszky that I first came across Hughes's version of Ferenc Júhasz's poem "The Boy Changed into a Stag Cries Out at the Gate of Secrets." I was struck by the fact that Hughes had made this version based solely on an English one by Kenneth McRobbie, and began to make a close comparison between his and McRobbie's version, in an attempt to find out what Hughes's alterations told us about his own poetic sensibility.

'During this work I happened to take a train to London. A stag party got on at York, and the carriage became, for a short period, territory ruled by them. Their terrible, eager, desperate faces produced in me feelings of interest, pity and fear. That occasion marked a time when as a poet I consciously wished to write about contemporary society. Júhasz's poem, written by a man in 1955 Communist Hungary, altered and conserved through many translations, suddenly appeared to me as a surprising, but wholly fitting model.'

LIZ BERRY was born in the Black Country and now lives in London where she works as an infant school teacher. She received an Eric Gregory Award in 2009. Her debut pamphlet, *The Patron Saint of Schoolgirls,* was published by tall-lighthouse in 2010. She is Emerging Poet in Residence at Kingston University and a 2011/12 Arvon/Jerwood mentee. She comments, 'I wrote "Sow" after catching a girl, who thought she was alone, stepping onto the weighing scales in the changing rooms and hissing at herself: "you fat pig". For days afterwards, I couldn't stop thinking about her and wanted to create a poem that would transform her into a little sow, sticking up two fingers, or four trotters, to the world. Her Black Country voice came first – "Trottering down the oss road in me new hooves" – and was a perfect fit, oinking its snout at the prissy standard. Once she'd starting speaking, she didn't want to stop – mouthing off about sex, food, men, femininity and all her irrepressible appetites. She was rebellious and rude, saucy and defiant, and I loved the sheer filthy abandon that she revelled in.'

ALISON BRACKENBURY was born in 1953. She has worked for over twenty years in the family metal finishing business. Her most recent collection is *Singing in the Dark*, Carcanet, 2008. Her eighth collection will be published by Carcanet in April 2013. New poems can be seen at her website www.alisonbrackenbury.co.uk. She comments, 'Manual work is often despised in England, with an almost religious fervour. I grew up in the gulf between two worlds. My father was a farm lorry driver, who, in my childhood, loaded and unloaded whole trailer-loads of sacks upon his back. My mother was a fastidious teacher. Curiously, it was my father's memory of a hot Lincolnshire classroom, in the 1930s, which led me to consider the world before deodorants. The past is a pungent country.

But I am not sure that a harsh miasma of chemicals is an improvement, especially if these have been tested in the eyes of animals. I spend my working days in my husband's family's metal finishing business. Our low workshop, even in summer, is heated by the ferocious gas burners under the vats. It is better not to look at the thermometer. I simply steam in my boiler suit. Much of my spare time is spent (some would say, wasted!) with our twenty-seven year old pony, who is kept on a farm on the hills. Her kindness is matched only by her magnificent indolence. After half an hour of persuading her to necessary exercise in the summer lanes, she arrives back cool as a cucumber, while I am dripping. So, in the new national religion of inactive cleanliness, both this poem and I must be classed as heretics.'

VAHNI CAPILDEO (Trinidad; UK) writes for the *Caribbean Review of Books* and the *Times Literary Supplement*, and volunteers for Oxfam. She recently completed *Utter*, inspired by her time working at the Oxford English Dictionary. Her third book of poems, *Dark & Unaccustomed Words*, appeared from Egg Box Publishing in 2012. She comments, 'The original "Wulf and Eadwacer" is a lyric in a woman's voice, composed in Old English and written up in the Anglo-Saxon period. The complex grammar of that language permitted the creation of a super-compressed poem, in terms of meaning. The pattern of sounds and rhythm, with their breaks and echoes, made for its mortal pulse. We can tell that the speaker is caught up terribly in a forbidden love; that there is physical separation, the stresses of confinement and of journeying, the thorniness of wood and peril of water; that there is armed conflict. It is very much a cry from a northern isle: the daily pain of physical loneliness; the infusion of the scene with rain and anger.

'The stakes are life and death, for woman, child and man. And so the puzzle of the super-compressed language sets itself up; draws us in. How many men are there: one, or two? Is the speaker addressing the lover, a husband, a guardian? How to appreciate, or resolve, the ambiguity of her expressions, when she uses words that could have double meanings: "gift" or "burden", "outlaw" or "wolf"? Can we link this poem to similar tragic, evocative fragments apparently in a woman's voice, or to other traditions, Latin or Scandinavian, to find a story?

'For years these words rushed inside me, muttering like a discomforting sea. I researched, and did not write, an academic paper. No-one could ever know, not for sure. Asked by Adam Piette and Alex Houen to contribute to a special "translations" issue of *BlackBox Manifold*, I naturally gave myself over once more to "Wulf and Eadwacer". Rather than pretending to make sense of the lyric, I tried to refract it, unpeel it; hence the mixed form, which airs the voices and concerns astir behind the surviving words, the enemies as well as the beloved. Readers wishing for a transparent, well-founded translation are referred to Richard Hamer's *A Choice of Anglo-Saxon Verse*.'

MELANIE CHALLENGER is the author of *Galatea* (Salt: 2006), her first collection of poems, and *On Extinction* (Granta: 2011), a work of non-fiction about our place in nature. She was Creative Fellow of the AHRC Centre for the Evolution of Cultural Diversity at University College London from 2007–2010 and International Fellow at the British Antarctic Survey. Her work was a recipient of the British Council Darwin Awards. She is now a research associate at Cambridge University's World Oral Literature Programme.

She writes, '"Suilven or *Humility*" is part of a longer sequence called "The Tender Map", which matches places and landscapes with some of the central feelings and responses experienced by us, inspired by Madame Scudery's map of emotion, "Le Carte de Tendre". This poem takes the striking mountain, Suilven, in the north-west Highlands of Scotland as its terrain alongside a positive sense of humility. The lovers climb the mountain, while time rolls away under their feet. Their love-making places them inside this same vertigo of time, part of the instinctive movements of nature, as the eagle, too, performs its perfect, unthinking action.'

AMARJIT CHANDAN has published six collections of poetry and two books of essays in Punjabi and two in English *Being Here* (The Many Press, 1993, 1995, 2005) and *Sonata for Four Hands* prefaced by John Berger (Arc, 2010). His work has appeared in *Modern Poetry in Translation*, *Poetry Review*, *Critical Quarterly*, *Wasafiri*, *Index on Censorship*, *Papirus* (Turkey), *Erismus*, *Ombrela*, *Odos Panos* (Greece) and *Lettre Internationale* (Romania). He was amongst British poets on Radio 4 selected by Andrew Motion on National Poetry Day in 2001 and has participated in the Alderburgh, Ledbury and King's Lynn poetry festivals. His short poem carved in 40-foot long stone both in Punjabi and its English version is installed in High Street Slough. He writes the following, 'It is an experiential poem. The poem came to be in Punjabi several years after the actual incident. I spent two years in solitary confinement for being an activist in the Maoist movement in Punjab India during the early 1970s. As a young poet I admired and envied great poets like Nazim Hikmet, Yiannis Ritsos, Faiz and many more who wrote great poetry in prison.

'Solitary confinement is the worst kind of punishment man can inflict on man. Time stands still. It is hard to pass the moment, the hour, the day. Yet years pass. Time irritates like chalk screeching on a blackboard. You count your breaths, lose count and start again. Thinking fills the emptiness, but too much kills you from the inside – the emptiness is infinite. My cell in Amritsar jail measured five of my steps by 10; it had six iron bars and was open to the elements. Punjab is a land of extremes, and so nature punished me as well. I slept on the floor, legs in iron fetters, with four coarse blankets over and under me.

'I remember vividly the day I was released. The gate was opened and I was out. I felt weightless. The noise and the smells of the city were both shattering and joyful. I was told that the image of walking on water alludes to Jesus Christ. I wrote what I had felt – nothing to do with megalomania etc. May be I was Peter seeking out Lord's hand. I was saved. The poem in the present tense and in the third person reads like a screenplay of a silent monochrome film and the scene is enacted as many times it is played on the memory screen. The imagery is mostly abstract and metamorphosed; only the feet and the earth underneath are solid.'

GILLIAN Clarke is a poet, writer, playwright, occasional translator (from Welsh), President of Ty Newydd, and the National Poet for Wales since 2008. Most recent collections: *At the Source,* a book of essays and a journal, and *A Recipe for Water.* a collection of poetry. In 2011 she received the Queen's Gold Medal for Poetry. A latest collection, *Ice*, is published by Carcanet.

She comments, 'For the past three years I'd been observing a pair of swans on the river Ely in Cardiff. They nested on the reedy shore of a little lake to the side of, yet joined to the river below the flat where I stay a few days a month. Every year the pair raised seven cygnets. In the long, bitter winter of 2010–11, from November to March, the river was frozen for months. Mute swans pair for life. When thaw came at last, the cob returned alone, re-building his ravaged nest. He was fierce and angry, defending his nest and his stretch of water for the return of his pen. She did not return. She must have been driven away by the ice in winter's confusion, and died. Had the surviving swan seen his mate's dead body, he could have accepted it, even, maybe, finding another mate eventually. The image of the dead swan, and the faithful, grieving widower swan seemed to need a noble image. The Mary Rose, Henry VIII's favourite warship, was sunk in a skirmish against the French navy almost 500 years ago. The poem needed to 'sing', with echoes and rhymes telling its sorrow.'

JOHN WEDGWOOD CLARKE is currently Leverhulme Poet in Residence at the Centre for Ecology and Marine Studies, University of Hull. He is co-artistic director of Sea Swim (*imove*), and UK and Ireland Editor, Arc Publications. He was founding director of the Beverley Literature Festival and Bridlington Poetry Festival. He holds a D.Phil. in Modernist poetics from the University of York. He comments, 'Sandside is the name of the road that runs around the inner edge of Scarborough's harbour, and the poem that bears its name is the opening part of a longer sequence titled *Scarborough Elegies*. The writing of the poem was guided by a long-buried sense of grief that surprised me as I wrote the words 'Don't go' and then found the rhythm of the first couple of lines. This discovery happened as a consequence of a morning spent making notes and poem sketches while poking around the harbour. I love harbours. I was born and raised in Cornwall. And now that I'd come to live in Scarborough I wanted to explore what this harbour might mean to me. When I subsequently went through my notes I found patterns of things – lobster pots, crab lines, gulls – that felt familiar and important. I let my growing sense of emotional urgency coupled with a loose sense of the sonnet form and iambic pentameter rhythm organise those things in a way that felt true. I like emotions and ideas spoken through things; I like a poem to accommodate as much of me as possible without explanation; I like a poem only to explain itself to my breath and my mouth. The ending describes a sense of possession through performance that I can remember experiencing as a child and which I saw another boy exploring as I walked the harbour that morning.'

JOHN CLEGG was born in 1986 and grew up in Cambridge. He currently lives in Durham, where he is finishing a PhD on the Eastern European influence in contemporary English poetry. A selection of his poetry was featured in *The Salt Book of Younger Poets*. His debut collection, *Antler*, is published by Salt. He writes, 'I keep coming back to those mermaids at the end of ". . . Prufrock", one of the all-time perfect metaphors, standing in for the society Prufrock can't help being pulled towards, knowing at the same time that it will suffocate him. I've tried to make my mermaids evolutionarily plausible, alien as much to themselves and each other as they are to us. The deep sea segment of David Attenborough's *Planet Earth* gave me some idea of the sort of life they'd lead: total darkness, total silence, shouldering a column of water the weight of a double-decker bus plus passengers. I'm not sure the pheromone language is actually possible, but then I don't suppose anyone would have believed in communication via black squiggles on bleached oblongs of woodpulp either, unless they'd seen it in action.'

DAVID CONSTANTINE taught German at the Universities of Durham and Oxford. He holds honorary professorships in English at the Universities of Liverpool and Aberystwyth. He is a translator and editor of Hölderlin, Goethe, Kleist and Brecht. He has published several volumes of poetry, most recently (Bloodaxe, 2009) *Nine Fathom Deep*; also a novel and three volumes of short stories. He was the winner of the BBC National Short Story Award 2010. With his wife Helen he edits *Modern Poetry in Translation*. He writes the following, 'The poem began in the fear of losing a particular "local habitation", a house by the sea. I suppose it widened then into a more general declaration of love for life and of loyalty to the here and now. The constituent details are local and personal, as they are very often in my poems; but I set them there in the hope that they would be lively enough for any reader to convert them into the stuff of her or his own life. It is quite a formal poem – because, in my view, form is an essential agent in the translation of the personal and local into the figurative, and so more readily into others' lives.'

SARAH CORBETT was born in Chester in 1970 and grew up in North Wales. She studied at Leeds University, the University of East Anglia and is currently completing a PhD in Creative Writing at the University of Manchester. She won an Eric Gregory award for poetry in 1997 and her first collection of poems *The Red Wardrobe* (1998) was shortlisted for a Forward First Collection Prize and the T.S. Eliot Prize. She has published two further collections with Seren Books *The Witch Bag* (2002) and *Other Beasts* (2008). She is currently working on a new collection of poems supported by an Arts Council England Writer's Award.

She comments, 'I wrote this poem in America, on a residency at Yaddo in 2005. Then promptly forgot about it. I only discovered it recently whilst going through some papers. What was interesting for me was how the form of the poem – a sort of free-hand blank verse – pre-figures a form I'm making use of in the collection of poems I'm writing now. I like the way I can stretch or compress the form to allow the 'walk' of the poem to find its distance. The poem is a real walk – you can follow it from Settle in the Yorkshire Dales in the general direction of Malham. However, the speaker loses the path through misdirection and a wrong turn and at the end of the poem she is only 'Half way back'. This does not matter of course, as the true direction of the walk has not been linear but inwards, towards a place of revelation. Although the poem owes debts to both Robert Frost and Gerard Manly Hopkins, but I guess the poem's true provenance lies in Wordsworth's great poem of walking and memory *The Prelude*. This is probably the first poem as a young student that I fully identified with. I've always been a wanderer and a walker, beneficiary of a rural setting and lax parenting in the early 1970s. I remain so today, and it's where I know I am fully myself and where the space opens up for poems to enter.'

ABI CURTIS's first collection *Unexpected Weather* was a winner of Salt's Crashaw Prize in 2008. Her second collection, *The Glass Delusion,* was published by Salt in 2012. She received an Eric Gregory Award in 2004 and holds a PhD in Creative and Critical Writing from the University of Sussex. She is a Senior Lecturer in English Literature and Creative Writing at York St John University. She writes, 'The poem explores, in part, the town where I grew up. It is in Essex and was more or less 'created' in the late 1970s as part of a move to develop certain areas, to encourage families to populate them. Apart from a small, old part of the town, this new community was built, with schools, a town centre, new streets and houses. There's something strange and artificial about this idea. At the same time, the town is built near a creek which flows into a river. This was a wild, salty, muddy landscape. We played there as children.

'Memory is deceiving, of course, so the poem deliberately takes this idea of a purpose-built town, ready to be populated, to a kind of extreme. I think it also reflects the idea of a very young population, buoyed up by possibility and opportunity, finding their way in this new environment which they see as belonging to them. But there are darker elements in the poem that reflect the scarier things that we tend to tune into when young. There is also that aspect of the natural world that resists the new population, defying their sense of having tamed a landscape. I wrote the poem whilst on an Arvon course, at Ted Hughes' once-home of Lumb Bank in Yorkshire; very far in time and space in terms of where the poem is set. The form is relatively loose, though the rhythm became a kind of chant, as well as a set of invitations to explore the town. I think the voice of the poem is strange: partly that of a child with a child's focus on certain details of their world, but also that of an adult reconstructing a memory.'

AMY DE'ATH was born in Suffolk in 1985 and studied at the University of East Anglia, UK, and in Philadelphia, US, before moving to Australia and then London. Her publications include *Caribou* (Bad Press, 2011), *Erec & Enide* (Salt, 2010), and *Andromeda / The World Works for Me* (Crater Press, 2010). Her work is featured in a number of UK anthologies. For three years she lived and worked in London, where she was recently also Poet-in-Residence at the University of Surrey. She currently lives in Vancouver, Canada, where she is studying for a PhD in contemporary poetry and theory at Simon Fraser University, and works on the poetics journal *West Coast Line*.

She comments, 'The poetry I love most – that I most want to write – is that which erupts from lived experience and is capable of spontaneity, 'un-knowledge' in freefall, happy accidents which show me "I" am not who I thought "I" was – and so allow me to step outside of myself. Alice Notley's sonnets, H.D.'s *Sea Garden,* or Joseph Ceravolo's *Spring in this World of Poor Mutts* offer a kind of expansion, play, pleasure in language that give way to a messiness and ecstasy sometimes lost in other modes of (dialectical, linear or perhaps deliberately programmatic) thought. At the same time I'm stuck on how poetic language is constantly and ever more inventively appropriated by popular (digital) culture – how can I begin to write my love poem when *Hipster Runoff* and *Vice* Magazine have already eaten it? I'm interested in how I might disregard or circumvent the limits of the conventional or depleted lyric in my efforts to be sincere, and in the work the rhetorical affect of a poem like "Failure" might accomplish. How can the kinds of pleasure and sincerity – perhaps the excess – I want from poetry be transformative; a form of affective politics?'

CHRISTINE DE LUCA (PEARSON) was born and brought up in Shetland, Scotland. She writes in both English and Shetlandic. Her fifth poetry collection, *North End of Eden,* was published in 2010 (Luath Press Ltd, Edinburgh). Active in translation, she has had poetry published in many languages and her trilingual Selected *Mondes Parallèles* (éditions fédérop) won Le Prix du Livre Insulaire, Poésie, 2007. She has participated in book festivals throughout Scotland and in Italy, France, Finland, Norway, India and Canada. Her first novel *And then forever* was published in 2011 (The Shetland Times). She writes the following, 'The stimulus for this poem came while walking across a particularly stunning beach in Shetland, near a geological "discontinuity" i.e. where you can set one foot on an ancient rock pediment and the other foot on an even older rock surface; hence the title of the poem. The emotional tension in the poem is built around this metaphor, likening this physical step to the spiritual/emotional step we take in relationships.

'The "heart" in the first stanza is also metaphoric. I had laid up one heart-shaped stone on a previous visit, but it had disappeared, perhaps taken by someone else or moved by the sea. So I laid up another one as suggested by the question at the end of this stanza. While the feelings expressed in the poem suggest reticence, the features of the natural world – the rocks, the wear and tear, the seashore birds (ringed plovers tripping along just avoiding the breaking waves) and the tides – are all upbeat about change, and thus potentially blameworthy for the emotional confusion. The final stanza tries to defuse the tension of the unspoken and infuse the moment with a beauty in ambivalence, as in the wave-break (da lönabrak). The poem could only be written in Shetlandic, my Mother tongue, so close is the relationship of land to language, of heart to homeland. It fell into simple stanzas, the rhythm sustained mainly by very short sounds, mainly monosyllabic words. This contrasts with the slowing towards the end and the rolling "r" sounds of "lönabrak" and the English "ultramarine", reminiscent of Reeves' watercolours. There is some internal rhyme to help hold it together and the natural onomatopoeic sounds of Shetlandic e.g. "vimmerin", "frush".'

MICHAEL EGAN is from Liverpool. His pamphlets are *Folklores, After Stikklestad* (both Knives Forks and Spoons Press) and *I Went to the Ship* (Erbacce). His first collection *Steak & Stations* was published by Penned in the Margins in 2010. He is currently working on a second collection, *Zenzizenzizenzic.* He comments, ' "Intermission" was originally a series of short connected haiku-like poems. It was part of a longer sequence called "Ampersand", poems that were all very abstract and yet in them I was trying to convey an over all story; a man wakes in a field and wanders the countryside searching for his wife. He writes, "Intermission" is a poem full of wandering thoughts and distractions. I remember writing the original poems that became "Intermission" in a small attic flat and listening to a neighbour playing his saxophone. It was a Saturday evening in Autumn and I wasn't going out anywhere. The neighbour was a terrible saxophonist but he wouldn't give up.

'"Intermission" is also a poem that reflects my interests in art, Norse mythology, surreal or unnerving snippets of stories or the over heard. I think there's something of *The Man Who Died* by DH Lawrence in it, something too of another book I was probably reading at the time which was *The Last Kingdom* by Bernard Cornwell. I would suggest that the poem is trying to convey something urgent and possibly sexual but ultimately I see it as a poem about interwoven narratives coming together at a point, the poem's end, that is both personal and mythologised; the vine wrapped tower is the house the flat was in, the forest is the park across from it, the nothing else is my boredom. Perhaps the urgency, tension, strangeness of it all represents my searching for a poem as I'm writing it, unravelling the subconscious and seeing how the words that are written down lead on into the next line or, as it was originally, the next poem.'

ELAINE FEINSTEIN is a prize winning poet, novelist and playwright. Her first novel, *The Circle,* (1971) was long listed for the 'lost' Man Booker prize in 2010. She has received many awards. including a Cholmondeley Award for Poetry, an Honorary D.Litt from the University of Leicester, and a Rockefeller Foundation Fellowship at Bellagio. Her most recent is *The Russian Jerusalem* (2008) for which she received a major Arts Council Award. Her versions of the great Russian poet Marina Tsvetaeva were first published in 1971 and have never been out of print. She has been a judge for most of the major literary prizes. She comments as follows, 'Last year, one of my sons discovered his favourite novelist, Dostoevsky, had a passion for Dickens. He began to read Dickens' novels, many for the first time, with mounting enthusiasm. I held off, a little. I had always loved *Great Expectations* and *David Copperfield*, but the dangerous caricature of Fagin in *Oliver Twist* troubled me. How could Dickens, so frequently a fighter for the underdog be so indifferent to the pitiable Jews who had taken refuge in London's East End ? Then, as I re-read *Oliver Twist,* I was bowled over by the living immediacy of Fagin and understood how Dickens could not resist him once he was imagined. I pondered on the amoral power of dreams, and my poem was born out of that.'

JANE FLETT is a philosopher, cellist, and seamstress of most fetching stories. Her first poetry book, *Quick, to the Hothouse*, is now available from dancing girl press and recent fiction has appeared on wigleaf, Bartleby Snopes and BBC Radio 4. Find out more at http://janeflett.com. She comments, 'This Cowgirl's Lament' is a paean to stepping down the left-handed path and embracing the whirlwind. Us cowgirls are always being told of the sensible steps – the shelves that need stacking, the degrees that need studying, the jobs waiting to be worked at – but their temptations always pale in comparison to the allure of the ranch. Of course, all that wayward galloping will earn you some bruises along the way. There'll be moments when you think of jettisoning your foolish daydreams and settling. Settling for, settling down. I wrote this poem to remind myself (and anyone reading) of the other option: to risk ridicule and pray for comets and peacocks, to keep spinning and bucking and hoping for the best. I also wanted to declare that "cowgirl" is a perfectly reasonable career plan. As is poet, for that matter. They beat the alternatives.'

JOHN GALLAS, born in New Zealand, shares his life between NZ and England. He has had nine collections published by Carcanet, with *Fresh Air and The Story of Molecule* due in mid-2012, and *52 Euros* (translations of a double A–Z of European poets) to follow in 2013. He writes, 'Out lonely tramping at the very north of the South Island of New Zealand, at the edge of Farewell Spit, I had this little supernatural adventure, which is All True and spooked me mightily. I found out about Taniwhas a month later: the tricks, the cave, the sea, the unaccountable moving of my plastic bottles, all was True. The poet had no option but to write, in appreciation of the reality of the Spirit.'

JOHN GOHORRY was born in Coventry in 1943, obtained an M.Phil at University of London in 1970, taught in FE and HE until 2006. He has published six collections of poetry, most recently *Samuel Johnson's Amber* (Shoestring, 2010) and *On the Blue Cliff* (Dark Age Press, 2012). He writes, 'The city in *Keeping the City* is Coventry and I wrote my poem out of a long sense of dissatisfaction with the dismissive stance taken towards Coventry by Philip Larkin, its most famous poet, in his poem "I Remember, I Remember". Unlike Larkin, whose poem ends "Nothing, like something, happens anywhere", I feel that a great deal happens, and happened, in Coventry, and my sequence (there are seven poems in all) celebrates some of the formative influences that the city has had on my intellectual and imaginative life.'

ANDREW GREIG, b. Bannockburn 1951, brought up in Anstruther, Fife, is the author of 19 books of poetry, non-fiction and novels. A full-time writer, he lives with his wife, novelist Lesley Glaister, in Edinburgh and Orkney. His website is at www.andrew-greig.weebly.com He comments, 'There are a number of Fife poems in my most recent collection "As Though We Were Flying", and "Wynd" is the longest. It reads like a preface to something, and may turn out to be (whether in poetry or prose, I don't know). I grew up, or tried to, in Anstruther in the East Neuk of

Fife. That small town, the coastline and the back-country and the people I knew there, all meant a lot to me, and I kept going back for many years after I had left. But it was only after the family house was finally sold, and I seldom had cause to go back any more, that it began to haunt me. That line of Neil Young's: "All my changes were there."

'When people die, or a place no longer exists as before, it may become necessary to re-make them within. This poem unspooled like a jerky film from the opening memory-image of overspill, and I went with that flow until it brought me to "Holly". I deliberately did not go back to Fife till these poems were done – it seemed this should be an internal reconstruction job, not historical research. So it is odd to now walk those streets and wynds again, where so many buildings are the same but their use and signs and inhabitants are not. Every phone box, corner, shop, pub and back lane comes with mood and moments and faces attached. One's adolescent past is so present and so gone, along with its stunning boredom and excitation. The aim in the writing is to resurrect and re-live it, sure, but also to better understand what was going on, because it shaped everything, and guides us still.'

VONA GROARKE has published five collections with Gallery Press, most recently *Spindrift* which was a PBS Recommendation in Autumn 2009. In the US, she publishes with Wake Forest University Press. She teaches in the Centre for New Writing at the University of Manchester. She writes, 'I live in Manchester: summer is often an abstract entity. You have to be grateful for just *not rain*. And yet . . . When summer slides into its ordained slot, the whole city leans into it, turns itself inside out. We take to our gardens; we turn out rooms and lives and voices to the open air. A summer day is every possible summer day made available to us, the ones we have already lived, the ones yet left to us. We live them playfully: wide-eyed, but with intent. Summer makes children of us. In my case, that requires a double take, through time and geography. My childhood was the West of Ireland: all my young summers cast aside there like rocks on Spiddal beach. In the poem, as in my garden, I plant English-sounding flowers, asters and peonies, betwixt and between the fuchsia and mallow of my Irish roots. Times, I don't know where I am, or very nearly. Two places and two notional homes: each opens to sunlight in the same way, and I live between them. My dream of home could be either home, the way midsummer faces exactly two ways: once towards what is already lost to us; once, (and more inventively), towards what is yet to come.'

JO HASLAM has been writing since the late 1980s. She has two collections and a pamphlet published by Smith/Doorstop and has had poems in many poetry magazines including *The Rialto*, *The North*, *Stand* and *Ambit*. She has also been successful in poetry competitions including The Plough, Yorkshire Open and *Mslexia*. In 2005 she was runner up in the National Poetry competition and in 2011 won joint second prize with Matthew Sweeney in the same competition.

She comments, 'This is one of a series of poems with the hart as a motif. Animals crept into my poems some time ago almost against my will. The dog was the first one; our own real dog who died but wouldn't go away. I found myself thinking and writing about him as I had never done while he was there. The hart poems were similarly triggered by a real creature; one that leapt across the road in front of my son close to the middle of a busy town. The first poem about this incident generated a number of others. At the moment there are six but there may be more to come.

'I started life as a painter and printmaker and am fascinated by those great observers and recorders of animals, Bewick and Audubon. After years of producing abstract paintings I returned to observational drawing and animals are marvellous subjects for that discipline offering all sorts of challenges of line, mass, movement etc. I am also interested in the animal as a symbol and the myths that surround those symbols. I tend to work on these "series" of poems very much as a painter does using a motif to reveal different aspects of that motif while at the same time using it to investigate varieties of form and technique. Before writing this particular poem I had been looking at and working on circular forms such as the villanelle and pantoum and while nothing like either of those I think the poem owes something to both.'

MICHAEL HASLAM was born in Bolton, Lancashire 1947, has lived near Hebden Bridge, West Yorkshire since 1970. Publications include *Continual Song* (Open Township 1986), *A Whole Bauble* (Carcanet 1995), *The Music Laid Her Songs in Language* (Arc 2001), *A Sinner Saved by Grace* (Arc 2005) *Mid Life* (Shearsman 2007), *The Quiet Works* (Oystercatcher 2009) and *A Cure for Woodness* (Arc 2010). Cholmondeley Award Winner 2011. Website www.continualesong.com. He writes, 'I want to say, out loud and Upper-Case, that the poems I make are Fictions of Verbal Exuberance, and to cap that with, And My Theme is Love, but as I rehearse the phrase I find I'm substituting "Emotional" or even "Erotic" for "Verbal". It is the words, however, that generate and ramify the fiction. The fictions often seem to work like oracles, exposing aspects of my predicament; and I hadn't meant to be confessional. I wanted to express Love.

'This "Love" seems to be threefold: Of Language, to be sure, but secondly: for an ordinary local place, its topography, history, flora, fauna, place-names and whatever. I like where I live: The Upper Calder Valley. Years ago I hit on a trick of writing place-names, actual or invented, in the lower-case: I like these self-descriptions drawn from a nigh-obsolete dialect. So: clough, sike, goit, laithe, slack, flaight, carr, and so on. May they live! But there was a third form of Love that now seems stuck like that dead tractor in Alder Carr. This is Lust, and thus Sexual Love (for the lasses, in my case, as it happens. Lust! Its ups and downs!) But alas, about the time I was qualifying for my bus-pass, I sensed that that lust's adventures had become a matter more of Memory than Prospect. "Old Lad" is clearly fiction. I am not a widowed farmer, and I know no such place as Croft Fold Farm, Nab Gate. One might think it says something about a retired labourer and failing poet, OAP, looking back on some past sad facts while inhabiting a moor-edge cottage, alone. I say again, No, it's simply Fiction, and I'm not as old as he seems, and, anyway, there's cheer in The Sepulchral Arms.'

PAUL HENRY is a Welsh poet and also a singer-songwriter. His publications include *The Brittle Sea: New & Selected Poems*, recently published by Seren in the UK and by Dronequill in India, under the title *The Black Guitar. Mari d'Ingrid*, a translation by Gérard Augustin of his fifth collection *Ingrid's Husband*, is available from L'Harmattan. *Excusing Private Godfrey*, his tribute to the playwright and actor Arnold Ridley, will be broadcast by BBC Radio 4 later in the year.

He writes, 'I imagine "Usk" will open my next book, in so far as it answers "Sold", the closing poem of my last collection, "Ingrid's Husband", which ends: "Where shall we put them, / the years, in our new house? / the years we are moving out of?" Whereas 'Sold' is concerned with a marriage on the edge, and the dangers of transplanting love into a different shape, "Usk" is about the consequences of cutting free. In this respect, it also answers a longer poem of mine from "Ingrid's Husband" called "Between Two Bridges", where the same river Usk runs through the poem but in Newport, rising and falling steeply between mud-banks, playing conveyor-belt to the city's junk and dreams. In "Between Two Bridges", a man is tempted by his teenage ghost to return to a village on the Usk, to "greener banks" and "clearer water, twenty years upstream." Some poems are prophetic and "Usk" is about the strangeness of becoming that ghost again, on the banks of the same river. It's a sad poem. Rivers play tricks on our lives. But it ends with hope and is essentially about becoming "renewed, transfigured, in another pattern", as Mr Eliot has it; like the river.'

SELIMA HILL grew up in a family of painters in farms in England and Wales, and has lived in Dorset for the past 25 years. *Violet* was a Poetry Book Society Choice and was shortlisted for all three of the UK's major poetry prizes, the Forward Prize, T.S. Eliot Prize and Whitbread Poetry Award. *Bunny* won the Whitbread Poetry Award, was a Poetry Book

Society Choice and was also shortlisted for the T.S. Eliot Prize. Her most recent collections from Bloodaxe are *The Hat* (2008), *Fruitcake* (2009) and *People Who Like Meatballs (2012)*. She comments, 'I don't know if it just because I am a woman or what but I seem to be motivated by shame – shame, for example, that I am a poet (so self-indulgent) and, paradoxically, shame that I am ashamed that I am. And such a bleak one. (And I think of myself as rather a jolly person!) But is it the duty of the writer to uplift? I do know one thing, a writer does not have a license to hurt people and I hope I never do. Perhaps that is why it is easier to write about elephants.

'Once I had written one elephant poem I wrote lots. (See *People Who Like Meatballs*.) It seemed to be a way of writing about the Buddhist idea of homelessness (sounds very airy fairy, I know), an idea I have always loved, probably without understanding it. And I like very small and very large things – including my dog (very large) and my house (very small). And best of all I like facts, so I mention *sturgeon* for example, not only because of the word sturgeon itself (complete with irregular plural) but also because of the fact that nephostromes are found in sturgeon and frogs but never in other viviparous animals except elephants.'

SHEILA HILLIER's first collection *A Quechua Confession Manual* was published in 2010 and shortlisted for the Aldeburgh Jerwood Prize. She won the Poetry Society's Hamish Canham Prize in 2009, was commended in the 2006 National Poetry Competition for her poem 'Pollux and Castor, elephants', and in the 2006 *Mslexia competition*. Her poems have appeared in *Orbis, Ambit, Agenda, Mslexia, Guardian, Brittle Star, Nth position, Poetry News, The Interpreter's House and anthologies*. She is Professor Emeritus of medical sociology at Barts and The London School of Medicine, and is a China and south Asia specialist in international health. She lives in London and Provence. She writes, 'When the Columbia shuttle disaster occurred in 2003 I could not write about the sight of the explosion or contemplate those who died. I did not think I could add anything to the sight of those bright spots of fire hurtling across the sky. I could only write in a 'slant' way by speaking about the physical impact of the tragedy back on the earth from where the shuttle had come. I wanted to convey something about destruction too, about the way that it can occur in small and particular ways rather than in one huge impact and how animals can be particularly sensitive to this. There are bizarre elements to the full story, where body parts and pieces of machinery were found over a wide area and souvenirs were originally offered on eBay. In the poem, my approach is forensic, the tone I strove for one of sobriety, leaving the reader to thoughtfully reconstruct the horror from the description of evidence retrieved.'

SARAH HOWE was born in Hong Kong in 1983. A former Foyle Young Poet of the Year, she won an Eric Gregory Award in 2010. Her pamphlet, *A Certain Chinese Encyclopedia*, is available from tall-lighthouse. Her work has been anthologised in *The Salt Book of Younger Poets* (2011) and broadcast on BBC Radio 3. She is a Research Fellow at Gonville and Caius College, Cambridge, where she teaches Renaissance literature. She writes, 'Last year I was commissioned, for a London event, to write a poem about a "dance craze". "Death of Orpheus" was the result of my near failure. Realising at last I would never manage a poem about the Macarena, I cast about for some alternative. I thought then of Euripides' *Bacchae* – its ecstatic chorus of Maenads dancing for Dionysus. With only a little sleight-of-hand, I decided these frenzied women were the *original* dance craze. From there, my mind darted to Orpheus, and the violent postscript to his failed rescue of Eurydice.

'According to Ovid, Orpheus is torn to pieces by a band of vengeful Maenads for scorning their love. They wrench off his head, which floats down the river Hebrus, still miraculously singing. I was caught by a detail in Ovid's account: the trees are so charmed by Orpheus's song they cast down their leaves to mourn him. I wanted my own poem to defamiliarise, disorientate – but only until the reader realises its narrator is a grove of observing trees. I found myself leaning less on Ovid or Dante than on contemporary poets who have imagined the mind of a tree – Jorie Graham's "I Was Taught Three", Peter Streckfus's "Event", Emma Jones's "Daphne". What would beings without feet make of dancing? "Death of Orpheus" took shape around a forest's perspective on the world: the collective pronoun, the continuous present tense, the string of ampersands. Being so long-lived, trees would experience time differently to us. Events would seem not so much sequential as laid out in space before them – a bit like Vonnegut's Tralfamadorian novels. Some actions – a dancer's steps, a man's disembowelling – would happen too quickly for them to perceive. They would feel Orpheus's suffering, but in their own treeish terms: the charcoal of his grief, his wooden lyre's wail. It became a poem about empathy – that dance of understanding and misunderstanding, as we project ourselves into the suffering other.'

JOANNA INGHAM's work has been published in *Ambit, Iota, Magma, The Mechanics' Institute Review* and the BBC's *Wildlife* magazine. She was Adult Runner Up in the BBC Wildlife Poet of the Year 2008 competition and won the Birkbeck Michael Donaghy Prize for Poetry in 2009. She has taught creative writing in a variety of settings including schools, museums, day-centres for older people and prisons.

She comments as follows, 'I wrote this poem after a walk near Grasmere in the Lake District. The weather was much as I describe it in the poem. Blossom on the trees gave an impression of spring but there was a sprinkling of snow and the wind was bitter. On the way round the lake, we came across an information board explaining that the flat boulder by the path was a "coffin stone" from the time when the dead from surrounding settlements would have to be carried to the church at Grasmere. As we walked on along the "corpse road", I began to imagine those other journeys. The poem wasn't originally a sonnet. It started out as a very short, rather impenetrable piece. Gradually, I came to feel that the subject matter demanded a sonnet. The sense of a "turn" inherent to the form helped me explore this turning point between winter and spring, death and life, past and future.'

ANTHONY JOSEPH is a Trinidad-born poet, novelist, academic and musician. He is the author of four collections of poetry and a novel, *The African Origins of UFO*s. In 2004, he was chosen by Decibel and the Arts Council of England as one of 50 writers who have influenced the black-British writing canon over the past 50 years. In 2005, he served as the inaugural British Council Writer-in-Residence at California State University. Los Angeles. *As* a musician he has released three critically acclaimed albums with his band The Spasm Band. He lectures in creative writing at Birkbeck College, University of London. His latest collection, *Rubber Orchestras* was published by Salt in 2011. In 2012 he represented Trinidad & Tobago at the Poetry Parnassus Festival at the South Bank.

He comments, '"River Dove" from *Rubber Orchestras* was inspired by Eduardo Galeano's epic *Memory of Fire*. Galeano's novel re-tells indigenous mythologies of Latin America as well as its colonial history. "River Dove" is – along with "River Mamba" and "Ground Dove" – part of a sequence of thematically-connected poems which deal with the effects of the colonial project in the Americas and draws its imagery and tone from this period. Like much of my work, the "meaning" of the poem is contained not in the linearity of thought or narrative but in the sound and the resonance of the images and metaphors. The poem presents the reader with a fragmented three stanza form in which the symbolic relation between the images gives the poem its synchronicity and thematic shape. This overall vibration/atmosphere is what is important here. Through the juxtapositions and leaps between stanzas and even within lines, I'd like the reader to feel a sense of movement in the process of deciphering and unravelling the texts. In this way, "River Dove" is typical of most of the poems in the collection. I wanted to create sculpture for the ear. To craft poems which were almost three dimensional and imbued with a physicality and a sense of improvisation, poems which "became" themselves when they were activated/read.'

ANNIE KATCHINSKA was born in Moscow in 1990, and grew up in London. She was a Foyle Young Poet of the Year in 2006 and 2007. Her poems have been in several anthologies including *The Salt Book of Younger Poets*, and her *Faber New Poets* pamphlet was published in 2010. She comments, 'Last spring some of my friends and I decided to do a "poetry swap" together, where we each wrote a poem and then gave it to another person without revealing who we were, like a secret Santa. The theme was "April Fool". I think this poem came out of the fact that I was actually feeling pretty foolish at the time – clumsy, muddleheaded, unreliable, stupid, sleepy, silent, spilling things and forgetting things and not knowing things, about to graduate and leave the country yet acting like a total child. Then I stumbled upon this word "Tawpie", which basically means "foolish or awkward young person", and so this poem happened.' She currently lives in Sapporo, Japan.

DAVID KINLOCH was born and brought up in Glasgow. He is a graduate of the Universities of Glasgow and Oxford and was for many years a teacher of French. He currently teaches Creative Writing and Scottish literature at the University of Strathclyde, where he is Reader in Poetry. A winner of the Robert Louis Stevenson Memorial Award, he is the author of five collections of poetry including *Un Tour d'Ecosse* (2001), *In My Father's House* (2005) and *Finger of a Frenchman* (2011), all from Carcanet. In the 1980s he co-founded and co-edited the influential poetry magazine, *Verse*. More recently he helped establish the first ever Scottish Writers' Centre and is a founder and organiser of the Edwin Morgan International Poetry Competition. His personal website is at www.davidkinloch.co.uk

He writes, 'My poem views the impending ecological apocalypse through the eyes of a slightly regretful giraffe. The idea for the poem came from reading a fascinating account of how Paris survived the great flood of 1910 by the historian Jeffrey Jackson (*Paris Under Water*, Palgrave MacMillan, 2010). Here I found a brief mention of what happened to some of the unfortunate animals stranded in the Parisian zoo, the *Jardin des Plantes*. Most were saved but it was all just too much for one of the giraffes. This episode caught my imagination but I knew nothing much about giraffes and felt that in order to create a possible voice I should find out more. I got hold of Lynn Sherr's charming account *Tall Blondes* (Andrews McMeel, 1997) which provided further inspiration. 'A Flood' is the first part only of a much longer poem which also features one of my giraffe's ancestors, an animal shipped to France in 1827 as a gift from Muhammad Ali Pasha of Egypt to Charles X. It landed in Marseilles and had to walk all the way to Paris. Needless to say, it has much to say about the state of the human societies it encounters on its journey. The poem issues finally in a "Mini Bestiary", a series of four line rhyming poems or squibs very loosely based on the French poet Guillaume Apollinaire's *Le Bestiaire ou Cortège d'Orphée.'*

JANET KOFI-TSEKPO was born in Portsmouth and grew up in London. Her poems have been published in *New Poetries V* (Carcanet), *Ten* (Bloodaxe), *PN Review*, *Magma* and *Poetry Review*. She studied English at the University of Manchester, took a multidisciplinary MA at SOAS, University of London, and more recently was one of 10 writers selected to take part in The Complete Works programme run by Spread the Word.

She writes, 'This piece was inspired by a photograph posted to an online writing group, in which members attempt the challenge of drafting a new poem a day each 30-day month of the year. The image of an arch reminded me of a fort built on the Gold Coast, now Ghana, used by the British as part of the Transatlantic Slave Trade. The archway at Cape Coast Castle, leading out to the sea, is taller than the average man. It's larger than one built at the neighbouring Elmina Castle several years earlier, which allowed little room for people to get through. At Cape Coast during this later stage, traders had found more systematic ways to prevent their captives from jumping into the sea on the way out from the dungeons to the ships. I imagine the narrator to be a young person when the story takes place, who hasn't seen much beyond his home environment. When he sees the ship at the end of the poem, he can only relate it to something he is already familiar with. I'm interested in those initial perceptions; our human tendency to ascribe to people or things a simplicity that doesn't exist.'

FRANCES LEVISTON's first book of poetry, *Public Dream*, was published by Picador in 2007 and shortlisted for the T. S. Eliot Prize. Her poems have appeared in the *Times Literary Supplement*, the *London Review of Books, The Times* and the *Guardian*. She works as a freelance poetry teacher and reviewer. She writes, 'In the Pitt Rivers Museum in Oxford there are ten shrunken human heads, also called *tsantsas,* collected between 1871 and 1936. The *tsantsas* were made in Ecuador and Peru by members of the Shuar, Achuar, Huambisa and Aguaruna tribes. Head-shrinking was a complicated procedure that involved removing the brain and skull, boiling the skin, and re-shaping the facial features as the *tsantsa* dried. Although the original murder was usually committed for reasons of vengeance, the ritual of preservation forged a kinship bond between the warrior and his conquest, inducting the soul of the victim into the warrior's tribe. The museum's curators have discussed at length the question of whether or not to repatriate the shrunken heads to South America. More information can be found at http://www.prm.ox.ac.uk/human.html.'

TIM LIARDET has produced eight collections of poetry. His third collection *Competing with the Piano Tuner* was a Poetry Book Society Special Commendation and long-listed for the Whitbread Poetry Prize and his fourth *To the God of Rain* a Poetry Book Society Recommendation. *The Blood Choir,* his fifth collection, won an Arts Council England Writer's Award as a collection-in-progress, was a Poetry Book Society Recommendation and shortlisted for the T.S. Eliot Prize. His pamphlet *Priest Skear* appeared in 2011 and was the Poetry Book Society Pamphlet Choice for Winter 2010; *The Storm House,* his eighth collection, was published by Carcanet in June 2011. He is Professor of Poetry at Bath Spa University.

He comments, 'Though I know it's the last plea anyone can make on behalf of a poem, *Deleted Scene (The Frog)* is rooted in experience. To my brother and I, still young, the frog was a mysterious force which appeared to be acting out a part, placed by us in a tin with a tragic *mise-en-scène* of rock, leaf and water. What surprised – and subsequently *haunted* us – was the frog's inability to save itself. It stayed put, trapped in its death-trance. It accepted its fate so completely it became for us a source of terror and guilt. Like the frog, though, we could do nothing; we were as helpless as it. Years later, after the death of my brother – who seemed when alive to act out his own personal tragedy – the memory of the frog remained. It began to assume a rich symbolism. This is one of two "Deleted Scene" poems to be included in *The Storm House.* They are so entitled because I have often come across outtakes hidden away in DVD special features that seemed like they should have been included in the original film. The title also implies something too painful to contemplate; something that so should not be shown, it has to be shown.'

FRAN LOCK is a sometime itinerant left wing activist, writer and illustrator, building a reputation on the London poetry circuit. Her work has previously appeared in *The Stinging Fly*, *Poetry London*, *Ariadne's Thread* and in Little Episodes' *Expressions of Depression* anthologies. Her first collection of poems, *Flatrock*, was published by Little Episodes, through Little, Brown in 2011. She has recently completed her MA in Creative Writing at Kingston University, for which she was awarded a distinction. She is currently editing her second collection, *The Mystic and The Pig Thief* and applying for her PhD. She writes, 'The pieces are extracts from a complete epistolary sequence, *The Mystic and The Pig Thief*, an imagined correspondence between two young people on the margins of Ireland's disintegrating traveller community, and the subsequent journal entries and letters sent by the young woman to others following the male protagonist's death. The reproduced sections deal with the travellers' eviction from the encampment at Smithy Fen in Cambridgeshire, the breaking up and burning out of the camp, and the female protagonist's flight to a communal squat in Croatia.

The finished work charts the irrevocable transition from nomadic life, through 'settled' communities, to a scattered existence on white working class sink estates. My protagonists stumble through this uncertain terrain, picking up scraps of tradition and folklore, flirting on the fringes of the new age "crusty" scene, ultimately though imperfectly absorbed in to "scaldie" life. The backdrop to these changes is Ireland itself, the widening gap between rich and poor; the increasingly random, increasingly apolitical gang violence, fuelled by clan feud and coke. The poems represent an attempt to address the fallout from these changes, both physical and psychological. "Pig Thief" loses his life to the flourishing culture of drugs and gun crime; "Mystic" leaves but struggles to make sense of her life in the face of her loss, and of an identity in rapid dissolution.'

RICHIE MCCAFFERY, 25, is a Carnegie scholar at Glasgow University researching the Scottish poetry of World War Two, towards a PhD in Scottish Literature. He has been a Hawthornden fellow and a recipient of an Edwin Morgan Travel Bursary. His poems have been appeared in such magazines as *The Rialto*, *Agenda*, *The North* and *The Dark Horse* and his pamphlet collection *Spinning Plates* is from HappenStance Press.

He writes the following, 'My poem 'Ballast Flint' was written in Cromarty in the lead up to a conference on Sir Thomas Urquhart, most well known as the translator of Rabelais. At this time, I was a writer in residence for the Cromarty Arts Trust and was drawing inspiration mostly from the immediate area and the stories of locals I encountered. On the shore is a ten-foot tall slate slab carved with the names of the emigrant ships that sailed from Cromarty for Canada in the early to mid 19th Century. The "Cromarty stone" looks like something between a totem pole and a giant gravestone and carries on it an epigraph from geologist and folklorist Hugh Miller which recalls how the crowds that saw off the ships waved and those on board returned their salute, but because of the wind and noise of the waves 'their faint huzzas seemed rather sounds of wailing and lamentation than of a congratulatory farewell'. Flint is a common feature on beaches nowadays due to its use as 'ballast' for empty ships, and in this poem I am drawing a parallel between the movements of flint via ships to that of the diasporic movement of emigrants as a result of "The Clearances".'

KAREN MCCARTHY WOOLF's pamphlet *The Worshipful Company of Pomegranate Slicers* was a *New Statesman* book of the year and a PBS recommendation. Her poetry is widely published, most recently in *Poetry Review*, *Poetry London*, *The Rialto*, *Magma*, *Modern Poetry in Translation* and in *Ten New Poets* (Bloodaxe, 2010). Karen has taught creative writing for a variety of agencies including the Photographers' Gallery, English PEN and the Arvon Foundation.

She comments, 'This poem forms part of a series of "cockney translations" commissioned by David Constantine as editor of *Modern Poetry in Translation* for an issue called the "dialect of the tribe" to celebrate language as an evolving, mutable entity, whether as regional dialect, patois or slang. My grandfather Charlie Robinson was born in Hoxton, east London in 1919 and died in Chichester in West Sussex on 1 January 2009, just four months shy of 90. All through our lives he was a consummate storyteller and would enthral the family with his tales of growing up in East London between the Wars. He was working class, poor and he and his brothers were taught to live on their wits.

'Not long before he died my mum had the foresight to get some of his stories down on tape. The thought of pressing 'play' was somewhat daunting but as it happened the warmth and booming cadences of his voice were hugely comforting and as soon as I started transcribing the material I knew that staying true to that voice would be a guiding priority. With this in mind, the poem uses loose rhyming couplets as a holding structure. Wherever possible I stuck to his original wording and story structure. Every time I thought about changing it I would usually defer to the original: he had the gift of the gab and there was little I could do to improve on it. This allegiance to voice is in a sense what makes the poem a 'translation' as the language is easily recognisable as English. The Hoxton he describes bears no resemblance to the cosmopolitan district populated by clubs, bars and boutique hotels that exists today. I hope that this poem will play its part in recording a unique aspect of London's cultural history.'

JAMIE MCKENDRICK has published five books of poetry including *The Marble Fly* (O.U.P., 1997), which won the Forward Prize, and most recently *Crocodiles & Obelisks* (Faber, 2008). He edited *The Faber Book of 20th-Century Italian Poems* and he has translated two novels by Giorgio Bassani, a verse play by Pier Paolo Pasolini and Valerio Magrelli's poems, *The Embrace* which won the Oxford-Weidenfeld Translation Prize and the John Florio Translation Prize in 2010. He comments, 'Moles have surfaced now in three poems of mine – somewhat to my surprise. Hedgehogs and foxes are more lovable, and more likely visitants in poems. Of course there are some mole poems such as John Bunyan's "Of the Mole in the Ground", which takes a dim view of its activities. There's the haunting American folk song "I Wish I Was a Mole in the Ground" sung by Bascom Lamar Lunsford, "The Minstrel of the Appalachians". And there's Kafka's relentless, terrifying story "The Burrow".

'The first I wrote, about ten years ago, referred to its cannibalistic habits; in a second, "A Mole of Sorts", it appears as an outsized dream-creature, a stand-in for death. So this third is maybe offering some redress: a more genial portrait of mole as regicide. The sight of a fresh molehill, a halo of soil on a snow-covered verge, reminded me of the Jacobite toast. Somewhere back of the poem is a memory of the largely post-sectarian Liverpool of my youth where I'd witnessed a small Orange march led by a bewigged, equestrian King Billy. Mouldywarp – literally "dirt-thrower" – is the archaic and northern dialect word for mole.'

MICHAEL McKIMM was born in Belfast and now lives in London. He is a graduate in English Literature and Creative Writing from Warwick University, an Eric Gregory Award winner and was 2010 British Council writer-in-residence at the University of Iowa's International Writing Program. The author of *Still This Need* (Heaventree Press, 2009), his work has appeared in anthologies and magazines in the UK, Ireland and USA including *Best of Irish Poetry 2010* (Southword Editions, 2009). Michael is a librarian at the Geological Society and is currently working on a collaborative project with earth scientists to create new poetic work addressing the geology of climate change.

He writes, 'This poem was written in the year my partner and I were planning our civil partnership and it documents four moments from our relationship: an impulsive excursion to witness the annual test of the Thames Barrier, a Mediterranean holiday, a period living in Coventry, seeking out its underground river, and our first visit together to the Giant's Causeway, on the north Antrim coast where I grew up. As well as being connected by water these scenes are also connected with moments or places of transition or crossing: a gateway in the act of opening, an underpass, a causeway. And, amongst other things, they are concerned with moments of breaking through, with emergence from hidden places, or (dare I say it?) coming out. I did not set out to write a sequence and there was a gap of some months between writing the different sections. Perhaps there are still more sections to come. On the other hand, the themes, images and locations are ones I've been playing with over and over in other poems (the title is a reference to an earlier poem, 'Fresh Water Cure', published in my collection *Still This Need*) so this does not feel exactly like its own poem – for me it is one part of the larger sequence of love poems that I have written and will continue to write.'

HUGH McMILLAN has had 5 collections of poetry as well as numerous pamphlets. He has been anthologized widely. He was a winner of the Smith/Doorstep Poetry Competition in 2005, the Callum MacDonald Memorial Award in 2009, and was shortlisted for the Bridport Prize and the Michael Marks Award in 2010. He was also a winner in the Cardiff International Poetry Competition in 2010. *Selected and New Poems* was published by Roncadora Press in 2012. He lives in Penpont in Dumfries and Galloway. He comments, 'Not much to explain here, what you see is what you get. My youngest daughter Jasmine was always complaining she never got much of a role in the annual Nativity play then landed the big one. It struck me that her confusion and stage fright maybe mirrored in a small way what Mary herself might have felt in the real event, if it happened. Also women have always occupied the very centre of the puzzle, even before Christianity. I don't belong to any faith – I had some debate about which word to use in the last line and plumped in the end for luck, as being more neutral.'

KATHRYN MARIS was born in New York and moved to London in 1999. She received a BA from Columbia University and an MA in creative writing from Boston University. She has won a Pushcart Prize, an Academy of American Poets award and fellowships from the Fine Arts Work Center in Provincetown, Yaddo and other artists' residencies. Her poetry, essays, interviews and book reviews regularly appear in British and American periodicals. *The Book of Jobs*, her first collection, was published by Four Way Books (USA) in 2006 and her second collection will be published by Seren in 2013. She writes, '"What Will Happen To The Neighbours When the Earth Floods" is an exercise in *ekphrasis* – that is, it is a poem that responds to a work of visual art. I wrote it as a gift to friends who hosted my book party at their gallery where a painting by British landscape artist Jacob More (1740–1793) caught my attention. I no longer remember much about the painting, which has since been acquired by the Tate, except that it's called *The Deluge* and depicts Noah, his ark, and various drowning figures, their faces conveying suffering.

'I had just started writing a series of God poems – the poems which constitute the bulk of my forthcoming collection – and this biblical subject fitted with my mode of thinking. But what was that mode of thinking exactly? I hardly know. This poem, written in 2007, was seemingly unpublishable until Kathryn Gray, former editor of *New Welsh Review*, found something worthy in it. Sometimes a poem's inability to find a home is an indication of its failure, and I am reconciled with the fact that some poems fail. But I believed in this poem. I reasoned that it was too odd, too "American" in style – and of course the God subject can be a turn-off in our secular world. I didn't give up on it. The problem, however, with such a long hiatus between writing the poem and writing *about* it is that I can no longer relate to it. What psychological state allowed me to identify with the wife of Noah, who narrates it? What does she mean when she says, "Sometimes I mistake Noah for God and sometimes I mistake God for no one"? She idealizes her man: she thinks he's God.

Or maybe, on the contrary, she's being ironic and she hates him. Maybe it's both. I used to know, but I don't anymore.'

HILARY MENOS was born in Luton in 1964, studied PPE at Wadham College, Oxford and worked as a journalist and restaurant critic in London before moving to Devon to renovate a Domesday Manor. Together with her husband, she set up and ran a 100 acre organic farm breeding pedigree Red Ruby cattle. Her first collection, *Berg* (Seren, 2009), won the Forward Prize for Best First Collection 2010. Her pamphlet *Wheelbarrow Farm* (Templar, 2010), was one of four winners of the Templar Poetry Pamphlet and Collection Competition 2010. She has four sons.

'*Bob's Dogs* is my homage to Welsh poet and clergyman R.S. Thomas, and is inspired by his poem *On The Farm*. "There was Dai Puw. He was no good." Thomas's poem challenges the cosy (English) view of the traditional pastoral poem with a stern but compassionate look at farm life in rural Wales,' she comments. 'My poem is rooted in fact. In 1994 I bought Bob's house – a dilapidated Domesday Manor – to renovate. Bob moved into the bungalow up the road. One of his dogs bit one of my builders, and then the postman. When the boy on the YTS scheme got bitten, the dog was shot.

'I wanted to write about this, about how it felt to be an outsider moving in to a close-knit community, and about farming. It is a harsh life (though not as grim in Devon as in Thomas's bleak Welsh hills). I wanted to show something of what it means to live on the land; the dirt, the various bonds between men and animals, and the occasional flashes of beauty. And I wanted to finish with something of the redemptive quality of Thomas's poem, though without recourse to religious belief. Thomas, understandably, disliked the intrusion of the English into Wales; Bob could have also resented the drift of Londoners down to the South West looking for a bit of rural idyll. But instead he welcomed "blow-ins" and reckoned we'd all get on with a bit of give and take. In my poem, "Bob" has come to represent the best of the old Devon farmers – resourceful, pragmatic, guarded but always ready to help, and wise enough to sit back and watch how things pan out, generally with a twinkle in their eye. Thomas goes out in a blaze of spirituality in his uncompromising poem. I find a rough and ready human wisdom at the end of mine.'

HARRIET MOORE is from South London and graduated last summer with a BA in English Literature from UCL. Her poems have featured in *Magma*, *Clinic* and *The Salt Book of Younger Poets* and are forthcoming in *Bird Book II* and *The Days of Roses Anthology II*. She now works for a literary agent and co-edits an arts blog and magazine. She writes, 'This poem began when the literary agents I work for had a spring clean. We were clearing out the bookshelves when I found *Bodies in the Bog* by Karin Sanders and became obsessed with it. Yet this is a poem about not being able to clear out, or be rid of. It is a waiting room. It is a space between. It is all your stagnant years or summers. I wanted to say, this is what happens when you get stuck, when you are heavy with the mud of losing something and not ready to dust yourself down. This is what happens when you can't pack something up and put it neatly away. This is all the mess that has escaped and can't be cleaned up quickly and put to bed. And of course this poem came from somewhere else too, a deep love for Hughes, and I suppose there is also some Heaney to be found in the bogland, as I could not have written about bogs without also somehow speaking through those men. It is their landscape and hopefully I have managed to cross it with the map they gave me and make it mine now too.'

KIM MOORE won an Eric Gregory Award and the Geoffrey Dearmer Prize in 2011 and has been published in magazines including *Poetry Review*, *The TLS*, *Poetry London*, *Magma*, *The Rialto* and *Ambit*. She is a winner of The Poetry Business 2011 Pamphlet competition, and her first pamphlet was published in spring 2012. She has recently finished an MA in Creative Writing at Manchester Metropolitan University and is currently working on her first collection.

She writes, 'When I wrote this poem, I'd just finished reading the novel *Jonathan Strange and Mr Norrell* by Susanna Clarke and the image of the drowned fields being another land comes from that novel. The landscape in the poem though is pure Cumbria, where I've lived for the last seven years – composed of the beach near where I live, and the fells where I walk – one day out hiking I found a massive hummock which the dog walked on and made wobble like a jelly, but when I walked on it (rather stupidly) I sunk up to my knees as it was full of water so this found its way into the poem. I'd also just got engaged, after never think-ing I would get married, and looking back now, I guess the poem was a working through of the feelings this brought up, although I don't think I realised this at the time. The other thing I remember reading and being struck by, which also found its way into the poem is a Rosemary Tonks poem where she says "He wants to make me think his thoughts/ And they will be enormous, dull – (just the sort/to keep away from)". The thoughts of the 'he' character in my poem are portrayed more kindly I hope.'

DAVID MORLEY is an ecologist and naturalist by background, his poetry has won fourteen writing awards and prizes. He is partly Romani and sometimes writes in that language. His next poetry collection *The Gypsy and the Poet* is forthcoming from Carcanet who have published his previous three collections. He teaches at the University of Warwick. He writes the following, "Ballad of the Moon, Moon' is a version of Federico Garcia Lorca's poem of the same name from his *Gypsy Ballads*. Lorca famously wrote of *duende* as a powerful, elemental style found in Gypsy songs and flamenco. The phrase "All that has dark notes has *duende*" is one of the engines of my writing about Gypsies, but it also drives my use of the Romani language. Romani possesses a music, an otherness and a wild precision that is understood by anybody who is alive and alert to the natural languages of the world. These languages might be registered as human speech, as birdsong, or as the movement of trees in the wind – or all of these, at once, in the moment of a poem.'

GRAHAM MORT's selected poems, *Visibility*, was published by Seren in 2007; *Cusp*, a new book of poems (Seren), appeared in 2011; *Touch* (Seren) won the 2011 Edge Hill prize for a collection of short fiction. Graham lives in rural north Yorkshire and teaches at Lancaster University where he directs the Centre for Transcultural Writing and Research and is Professor of Creative Writing and Transcultural Literature. He comments, '"Passed" is a poem that haunted me for a long period, but took a relatively short time to write. I've reached the middle age where a lot of the people I know – parents, colleagues, friends – are now dead. It's strange – perhaps inevitable – that they remain in my consciousness as if they were still alive. At least, they are as alive as they were when I wasn't in touch with them, but knew that they were "out there". That presence, perhaps the origin of the sense of being of "haunted", is most powerful in dreams when time and place dissolve into surreal interactions and a curious sense of intimacy. The dead are lodged in our consciousness, which brings them to life, just as it does any remembered experience, or any person or place that we think about or construct through the imagination when we aren't in direct contact.

'The poem is partly about sleep, too, the amazement of waking to oneself again (to paraphrase Edward Hirsh's poem "For The Sleepwalkers") with a loved other who is both intimate and ultimately unknowable because their own dreams and consciousness are just that – their own. The poem arrived quickly when I began to type and I choose a headlong form with a slightly jerky, incremental rhythm, abandoning left-hand justification to spring the lines into each other until that last word, with its faintly echoed rhymes and allusion to departure. Poems, like people, are also both familiar and unknowable, having both a conscious and unconscious manifestation. They are invocations, with their roots in myth and ritual, so desire, experience and imagination meet there. I guess this is as far as I'd like to go towards introducing, but not explaining, anything I've written!'

STEPHANIE NORGATE's radio plays have been broadcast on BBC R4. Her poetry publications include: *Fireclay* (Smith Doorstop pamphlet 1998), *Oxford Poets 2000* (Carcanet 2000), and *Hidden River*, (Bloodaxe Books 2008) shortlisted for the Forward First Collection and the Jerwood Aldeburgh First Collection prizes. Her second full collection, *The Blue Den*, is forthcoming from Bloodaxe in September 2012. She runs the MA in Creative Writing at the University of Chichester where she has taught for sixteen years.

She writes, '"Free Style" was commissioned to celebrate the month of September. The occasion of the poem stems from meeting friends to swim in the local river. As a lecturer, I am painfully aware that the "free" experience of writing and reading is no longer free for those who choose to study these arts. My friend's teenage daughter had recently returned from months away in hospital with a serious illness. After attending a long staff meeting about fees and "value", I saw her swimming again on a late September afternoon, and this meshed thoughts about differing kinds of freedom and values – free verse, wild swimming and the freedom of the trout in the river to continue their existence. The challenge in this case was to keep the poem deliberately loose and free (with no reductive workshop-style cuts), to allow the intended repetitions to stay, and to allow the syntax to follow a meandering line of thought in order to create emotional connections in the final periodic sentence. The poem expresses a hope – for a successful homecoming, for a natural co-existence with the world's flow, for the ability to enjoy free experiences, such as swimming, writing and friendship, before the winter comes on.'

BERNARD O'DONOGHUE was born in Co Cork in 1945. He moved to England in 1962 and has lived in Oxford since 1965 where he is now a teacher of Medieval English at Wadham College. He has published six books of poems of which the most recent is *Farmers Cross* (Faber 2011). Of his poem Sardines, he writes, 'I am thinking of that children's game "sardines" in which one person hides and each of the seeking group hides with them as they find them, until there is only one seeker left. The "he" that is being sought in the first line here is a mixture of two things: the original imaginative subject to write about; and, roughly, God – the deity that was the original transcendent figure, now lost or hidden. (I suppose the grand term for it is "deus absconditus" – but that is a bit too grand!) The middle stanza lists some of the occurrences of the deity in a Catholic childhood. And the last stanza hints at some vague figure of the numinous that maybe still exists in the imagination, though out of reach – and maybe only accessible to the individual.'

RICHARD OWENS is the author of *No Class* (Barque Press 2012), *Ballads* (Habenicht Press 2012) and *Clutch* (Vigilance Society 2012). He edits *Damn the Caesars*, a journal of poetry and poetics, and Punch Press. He comments, '"Immigrant Song" is a ballad. Although the ballad as a genre extends back to at least the late medieval period and possibly earlier, it is with the emergence of capital and the modern nation that ballad production becomes a site of fierce contestation and struggle. Through major canon-forming collections like Thomas Percy's 1765 *Reliques of Ancient English Poetry*, a work that was especially dear to Wordsworth and Coleridge, and Francis James Child's 1882 *English and Scottish Popular Ballads*, specimens of the genre have been framed through an almost tribal sense of national belonging. Even in twentieth century collections curated by seminal figures such as Alan Lomax, ballads scarcely ever surrender the flags they carry. When they do it is all too often in exchange for another flag. Nor can we know how many ballads trickled down to common people from the privilege of royal courts and bourgeois parlours through a specifically cultural form of supply-side economics. In this way, the ballad appears to function more as an instrument of power than any *völkisch* testament to older ways and better days. Poetic re-appropriation, however, has often enabled the remediation of ballad practice, and many poets since Wordsworth have likewise struggled to reimagine the genre, including Thomas Hardy, Helen Adam, Robert Duncan, and, perhaps most recently, Tom Pickard. In so doing, each of these poets call us toward the etymological grounding of ballad practice in the movement of the body – as in the Old French *balete* or *ballaite,* where the graceful precision of modern ballet is shattered against the raucous splendour of amateur night at the local bar.'

RUTH PADEL's latest collections include *Darwin – A Life in Poems* and *The Mara Crossing*, a meditation on migration in birds, animals and people in the "mixed form" of the *prosimetrum*, interweaving poems with prose. She is Fellow of the Royal Society of Literature and Zoological Society of London, and presents BBC4's *Poetry Workshop* on writing poems. Her works on reading poems include *The Poem and the Journey*, *52 Ways of Looking at a Poem* and *Silent Letters of the Alphabet*, her Bloodaxe Lectures on poetry's use of silence. See www.ruthpadel.com.

She comments, 'I wrote this poem when my daughter was finishing university and heading out into the world. I became the introductory poem to my book on migration, *The Mara Crossing*. This book took seven years, it has ninety poems threaded through with prose, and during those years I realized that writing about migration is also writing about home. Leaving home, losing it, making one again, re-finding home in yourself. I came to see every transition, such as growing up, in migration terms.

Some of the imagery comes from a story about wild horses, *Green Grass of Wyoming* by Mary O'Hara, which I used to love as a child. Because of this wild horse imagery, I first called the poem "Lone Ranger": from my favourite TV programme when I was 6. I was picturing the growing self, I suppose, as the rootless hero, moving on alone. The programme always ended with someone asking, "Who *is* that man?" "He's the Lone Ranger," they replied. That title was a sort of joke, but the poem seemed to me to be about courage, the courage of moving on and going further. Later, having realized that one theme in the work I'd been doing so long was "new life" (title of my poems–cum–prose model, Dante's *La Vita Nuova*), I changed the title of this poem to switch the focus from the speaker to what is discovered.'

ALASDAIR PATERSON was born in Edinburgh and lives in Exeter. He only recently returned to writing after a 20-year gap, during which he directed the work of several academic libraries in Britain and Ireland and travelled extensively. He won an Eric Gregory Award in 1975; his latest full collection is *on the governing of empires* (Shearsman).

He writes, 'In 1986, before moving to an Irish university and finding myself totally absorbed with budgetary issues, personnel conundrums and campus politics, I had been getting interested in the French Revolutionary Calendar and in particular *Brumaire,* the misty month; before I retired at the end of 2006 I found myself reading the business papers of a family who, living in revolutionary Paris, logged the old routines of getting and spending under the new names for the months. I began to think about the hazards of ordinary lives lived in such times of upheaval, among the savageries and bureaucracies of galvanic change. The daily news was, after all, full of them. Then I made the further discovery that what had originally been proposed by Fabre d'Eglantine (a poet, perhaps inevitably) and his revolutionary committee in 1793 was nothing less than a complete renaming of all the days too, with every day given a unique name culled from nature and agricultural life. Strangely, these never caught on . . . I wrote poems about a dozen such days in Brumaire; *Pomegranate* was the name given to the 19th day of that month (otherwise the 9th November), and I was attracted by the comparative exoticism of the fruit and the echoes of the story of pomegranate seeds and the daughter lost in the underworld in classical myth. Scenes of books in danger also seem to exercise a strange fascination . . .'

ANITA PATI was born and grew up in a northern seaside town and now lives in London. She has trained as a journalist and a librarian and was a 2011 Jerwood/Arvon poetry mentee. 'An unborn child wonders if it's worth it' is her first published poem, appearing in *Magma* in 2011. She writes, 'I was thinking about dialogue poems and these two voices came to me pretty naturally although I suspect there were other voices in there too. The premise is quite simple and explained in the title: should this child come into the world, with all its scariness and all its beauty? I wanted the voices to be migratory over time and space, after all, this child's voice could come from any soul. The voice picking up its concerns – the voice in italics – could also be any gender, anyone, perhaps a potential parent but not necessarily. Some of the language and imagery hopefully reflects both the child's clumsiness of speech and the startling clarity that children can exhibit. There is no real resolution.'

ELEANOR PERRY lives in Canterbury and is studying for an MA in Creative Writing at the University of Kent. She has recently been awarded a Graduate Teaching Assistantship by the University on completion of the MA. In addition to writing poetry, she also has an interest in the process of poetry translation, which will form a large part of her PhD research. Previous work has appeared in *The Delinquent* and *Timbuktu Magazine* and in 2011 she won the Faversham Fludde Festival Poetry Competition alongside eight other poets. She comments, ''Sole' is part of a short series of poems written in the summer of 2011, and based on my experiences in the town of Folkestone, Kent. All of the poems in the series explore the peculiar mixture of beauty and ennui inherent in certain British coastal towns. Folkestone in particular has an intriguing liminal quality, since it balances on the threshold between dereliction and regeneration, and my aim was to capture this as much as possible in the language used. The poem incorporates a lot of culinary imagery, since I was working at a local seaside restaurant at the time. I was fascinated by the gulf that exists between the wealthy clientele and the local people who live and work in the town, and I feel this is reflected in the poem. Each of the poems in the series is named after a sea area from the shipping forecast.'

PASCALE PETIT's latest collection, *What the Water Gave Me: Poems after Frida Kahlo* (Seren, 2010), was shortlisted for the T.S. Eliot prize, Wales Book of the Year, and was a book of the year in the *Observer*. Black Lawrence Press published an American edition in 2011. She has published five collections, two others of which, *The Huntress* and *The Zoo Father*, were also shortlisted for the T.S. Eliot prize. In 2004 the Poetry Book Society selected her as a Next Generation Poet. She tutors poetry courses for Tate Modern.

She comments, 'This poem is from a new collection I'm working on about my birth city, Paris, and was written there. I started it when I bought a book of María Sabina's curing chants from L'Harmattan bookshop in the rue des Écoles. María Sabina was a Mazatec *curandera* and I wanted to match her curing with my estranged and dead father who had harmed people, so in the poem it is him speaking. He speaks from the dead about the places he visits, just as Sabina used to journey to upper and lower worlds in her trances. I tried to keep to the "song" of her chants, but lost my nerve so abandoned the poem. A year later when *Magma* asked me to choose a presiding spirit for a commissioned poem for their feature I returned to Paris and tried again.

'I discovered that for years my father had lived in hotels opposite Notre Dame cathedral, that the chimeras and gargoyles of the towers would have overlooked him, and when I climbed up the towers I was struck by how alive these creatures look, like an aerial limestone zoo. I have developed an obsession with Notre Dame's exterior and regularly visit Paris now, staying near the Seine in the Latin Quarter to research and write. In the poem my father goes up the towers, becomes a chimera devil and a stone angel, and he descends to the cellars and jazz-caverns of the medieval Paris streets. He was part of the fifties jazz scene and its cavern clubs and I had been put in cellars as a child, so the underground city fascinates me; this part of Paris has an intricate network of ancient tunnels. This is the first time I've written extensively about a European city, as my usual habitat for my poems is wilderness.'

JACOB POLLEY has published two collections of poetry with Picador, *The Brink* and *Little Gods*. His novel, *Talk of the Town*, won the 2010 Somerset Maugham Award. His new collection, *The Havocs*, is due out in 2012. He teaches at the University of St Andrews and lives in Fife. He comments, 'This poem is odd to me and might be odd to a reader. I wrote it and rewrote it in a kind of lunacy and frustration. I had an urge to address the moon, and to make it symbolic, but I was also made mad and impatient by this urge. Perhaps the moon is an old, unusable, soot-grimed thing, and any words addressed to it are old, too. A lover can sometimes demand – sometimes of himself or herself – that something be said that is newer, clearer and truer than what's been said in the past, and I suppose a maddening delight in this impossibility might also lie behind the poem.'

CAROLINE PRICE was born in Middlesex in 1956. She studied Music and has worked as a violinist and teacher in Glasgow, London and Kent, where she now lives. She has published short stories and three collections of poetry, the most recent of which is *Wishbone* (Shoestring Press, 2008). She writes the following, 'I first drafted this poem during the unseasonably warm April of 2007 while I was staying at the Villa Marguerite Yourcenar, a residence for European writers in northern France. The park which surrounded the Villa was open to the public and very popular as a place to relax in, especially at weekends. My room had a wide view over the park and the flat landscape beyond, often shrouded in mist in the early mornings. And on Mondays, if I woke early and looked out of my window, I would see an elderly man with a long pole making his way through the park, up and down the footpaths: he was employed to clear up any rubbish left after the weekend. He cut a ghostly figure, emerging from the mist, and it was impossible not to think of the spectre of Death, particularly in that Flanders setting, among the battlefields of the First World War. He seemed so clearly to symbolise the passing of time, the clearing away of each generation to make way for the next.

'My intention in the poem was not to convey a bleak or particularly sad mood but rather a philosophical acceptance of death and the sense that we are all part of life which is constantly renewed and which will go on regardless. The form came quite naturally at an early stage: the long lines and the three-line stanzas felt appropriate for the fluidity and momentum I wanted to capture, as did writing the poem in one long sentence. And the use of the construction *After* . . . right at the beginning, with its implication that something else is about to happen, and that that something will be explained, hopefully acts as a device to attract the reader's interest and draw them through the poem.'

Raised in Virginia, ANNE ROUSE worked in the NHS and for a mental health charity after reading history at the University of London. Since 1995 she's been a freelance writer and lecturer, with Royal Literary Fund Fellowships and other residencies in Glasgow, Belfast and London. Her poems have appeared in anthologies in Britain, the USA and Canada. Her latest collection is *The Upshot: New and Selected Poems* (Bloodaxe, 2008). She writes, 'Although the poem ends in the present, the speaker is recalling an earlier, less eventful time. Her life has changed entirely. From an urban, indoor, rather isolated existence she's fallen into the opposite: she's gone over the wall, so to speak, and can now see, working on the beginnings of a shared garden, what has clouded her outlook in the past. "High Wall" is what I call a gateway poem, where a private breakthrough is being signposted or foreseen. More generally, it aspires to be a lyric poem, lyric poetry being a crucible in which consciousness – fragmented in myriad ways, including by language itself – achieves a momentary unity. Finally, it's a personal account, a story told by one friend to another. Like the title, the form and imagery are fairly simple, because the experience they convey, the overcoming of inner limitations, is both ordinary, and universally human.'

KATHRYN SIMMONDS was born in Hertfordshire in 1972. Her collection *Sunday at the Skin Launderette* was published by Seren in 2008 and won the Forward Prize for best first collection. She lives in London with her husband and baby daughter, and is working on a second book of poems. She comments, 'When this poem was written I was tutoring a poetry workshop at Morley College. To keep everyone writing, I would set a homework exercise for the class, the results of which they'd read the following week. Low on forms we hadn't tried, I brought in some examples of the ghazal, a lyrical Persian form which incorporates a mono rhyme and a refrain. Assessing the task ahead without enthusiasm, one mischievous lady in the group insisted I join in the exercise, so with a heavy heart I went home and switched on my computer.

'It took a few false starts before the poem began to appear, and a lot hinged upon finding the right refrain – which in my ghazal is the expression 'my dear'. This phrase set the tone, and once I'd found the opening line, (which owes something to the spirit of Auden's "Musee des Beaux Arts", another poem we'd been looking at, that idea of suffering occurring as life carries on), the poem took on its own momentum. It was spring 2010, we'd just been through the slightly depressing coalition process, so that's I think why *quid pro quo* comes up. The reflective narrative voice seemed able to accommodate both the public and the private, but writing poems is a strange business, and all sorts of things manifest. I never set out to write this poem, but perhaps sometimes a little of what you don't fancy does you good. My thanks to Patricia Hann.'

ZOË SKOULDING's most recent collections of poems are *Remains of a Future City* (Seren, 2008), long-listed for Wales Book of the Year 2009, and *The Mirror Trade* (Seren, 2004). She lives in north Wales, where she lectures in the School of English at Bangor University, and has been Editor of the international quarterly *Poetry Wales* since 2008. She writes, 'This poem began in January 2010 when I happened to be staying in Moynes Court near Chepstow, once the residence of Francis Godwin, who was then Bishop of Llandaff and later the author of the 1638 work of science fiction *The Man in the Moone*. His intriguing narrative reveals not only that the inhabitants of the Moon take advantage of the low gravity to travel around propelled by fans, but also that they communicate through a wordless musical language. As well as the title of the poem, the last two lines of the second section are taken from Godwin. However, I was also thinking about more recent discoveries, like the traces of our planet found on the Moon that suggest an originating collision, or the curious fact that the Moon moves away from Earth each month at about the rate as a fingernail's growth. The poem travelled with me under moons of 2010 in Nicaragua, Luxembourg, Sète, Istanbul and north Wales; it was orbiting my reading of Denise Riley's *Impersonal Passion: Language as Affect* and poems by Hélène Dorion, and it was there while I was translating poems by Jean Portante. It was finished in November, in time for the Colloquy of Poets at the Philip Larkin Centre, Hull University, which had commissioned a poem to mark the event. I first read it there, although it has very little to do with Larkin.'

Linus Slug is a London based poet, founder of the *ninerrors* poetry series and editor of *FREAKLUNG* poetry zine. Investigating identity through poetic practice, the work references Northumbrian history, and North-Eastern dialect as well as insect folklore and mythology. The idea of containment is explored through self-defined boundaries in the form of the nine-line poem, examining the tension that exists between the interior and exterior "self". Work can be seen in *Cambridge Literary Review*, *Veer About* and *Cannibal Spices*, and in *Better Than Language* and *The Other Room Anthology*.

Linus writes, 'wulfmonath is the opening section from *Reckoning*, a longer sequence of poems which alludes to *The Reckoning of Time*. Written in 725 by the Venerable Bede, a Northumbrian monk and early English Historian, *The Reckoning of Time* describes a variety of ancient calendars, including the calendar of the Anglo-Saxons. Wulfmonath or Wolf month was the name given to January among the Angles and Saxons - the time of year when wolves were bold enough to enter villages, driven by hunger and lack of food: "wading through the human / swirl mute as shadow". *Reckoning* tells an imagined Northumbrian history, playing on ideas of myth or legend in which characters are represented as insects; for example, in wulfmonath the Border Reivers are depicted as *Musca domestica*, more commonly known as the housefly: "living + feeding on / garbage + faeces like," – in later parts of Reckoning we meet "Elbowed Red", a common red ant and *Calosoma inquisitor*, a species of ground beetle. Although *Reckoning* begins with wulfmonath and follows the calendar chronologically, the sequence itself continually shifts back and forth throughout time, mapped by references to past and present-day; alternating between Border Reivers (late 13th to early 17th Century raiders, celebrated in Border Ballads) contemporary musicians (Pagan Wanderer Lu and Leafcutter John) and Icelandic Skalds (medieval Viking poets). Entomological vocabulary and North Eastern dialect occupy the same space, adding to a sense of displacement in this re-imagined folk tale.'

Anne Stevenson is an Anglo-American poet who has lived and worked in Britain for fifty years. Her many collections of poetry include *Correspondences* (1974), *The Fiction Makers* (1985), *Stone Milk* (2007) and *Poems 1955–2005*, published by Bloodaxe Books in 2005. The author of two critical studies of Elizabeth Bishop and a biography of Sylvia Plath, she has received among other prizes, a Lifetime Achievement Award from the Lannan Foundation and The Neglected Master's Award from the Poetry

Foundation of America. Her sixteenth collection, *Astonishment*, will be published by Bloodaxe Books in late 2012.

She comments, 'When I was ten my piano-playing father presented me with a cello we jokingly named Caesar, and during most of my school years in the States I burned with ambition to become a professional musician. My cello teachers, Mr. Troostewick in New Haven and Mr Edel at the University in Ann Arbor, encouraged me, but, suspecting that I could never become more than a mediocre performer, I switched my course of study from music to literature before I graduated, and at twenty-one I gave up my musical ambition in order to marry and become a school-teacher in England. Naturally, I took my cello with me and even gave cello lessons until, at about thirty, I began to notice people looking at me oddly, sometimes making faces when I played. So I took myself to an audiologist who confirmed my worst fears; I was going deaf, and nothing could be done to halt the process. Fitted with a hearing aid, I managed – just – to teach and converse normally, but it soon became evident that music now sounded to me, as my deaf sister put it, "like so many nails falling into a bucket". It was at this point that I discovered that the music I could no longer physically hear was still active in my memory, in my inner ear, and that it had undergone a kind of metamorphosis to become the rhythmic foundation of the poems I began to write in the early 1960s. Poetry had up to then been for me a secondary vocation, a release from the disciplines of music; it now became central to my life, confirming my inability to escape the demands of art. What luck that my deafness prevented me from even trying to become a cellist! The play on the word "left" at the beginning and end of this sonnet is deliberate; for poetry, which I'd assumed to be a kind of left-over vocation, turned out after all to be the right one.'

GRETA STODDART was born in Oxfordshire in 1966. Her first collection *At Home in the Dark* (Anvil) was shortlisted for the Forward Prize for Best First Collection and won the Geoffrey Faber Memorial Prize 2002. Her second collection *Salvation Jane* was shortlisted for the Costa Book Award 2008. Her poems have been published in many newspapers and magazines including the Independent, the Spectator, Poetry Review and the TLS. She is a poetry tutor for the Poetry School and the Arvon Foundation. She lives in East Devon.

She writes, 'The story referred to in the first line is *The Subtle Knife* by Philip Pullman. He was my teacher at school, and he used to write these fantastic plays for us. One thing I love about the theatre is how it's a world within a world, and how acting is about performing in one world while being in another. People close to me have died and I have had a strong sense of their having gone into another world. In the poem you get into that other world through the split in a stage curtain. As a performer I often had a profound dread in the wings, before I went on, and the relief afterwards, of being back in the wings, was equally strong. The time on stage evaporated into a kind of fierce, bright, fleeting present. I think this poem is partly about the ordeal of performance, of life. It's also a small fantasy of how it might be when that performance ends. Why tercets? – the poem quite quickly had that pulling back and forth feeling, one step forward, two steps back, wanting and not wanting, there and not there, being and not.'

CLAIRE TRÉVIEN was born in 1985. Her debut pamphlet *Low-Tide Lottery* was published by Salt in 2011 and her first collection will be published by Penned in the Margins in 2013. Her poetry has been published in several magazines and anthologies, most recently *Lung Jazz: Young British Poets for Oxfam* (Cinnamon Press). She is the editor of Sabotage Reviews (http://sabotagereviews.com). Her website is http://clairetrevien.co.uk

She writes, 'The inspiration for this poem came from watching a show on the Franco-German channel Arte with my grandmother. A violin's body was being described as being a woman with shoulders and hips. This image haunted me and seemed like a particularly useful vehicle for creating a feminist-agenda poem without alienating readers. The phrase 'Violins steal the voices of women to put in their cage of shoulders and hips' quickly imposed itself. I played with this idea in a more traditional format at first. I wish I could pinpoint the exact moment that I decided to transform it into this shape, but I'm afraid that that is lost in the tunnel of time. All I can say is that it took many more drafts for it to arrive at this present stage. I think the piece works particularly well as a performance piece, with the audience reading the left-hand column as I answer them with the right-hand column. The quasi-chanting they achieve as they encroach upon my lines adds resonance to the piece. Try it.'

MARK WALDRON's first collection of poems, *The Brand New Dark*, was published by Salt Publishing in 2008; his second, *The Itchy Sea*, also with Salt, followed in 2011. He's been widely published in magazines and his work appears in *Identity Parade: New British and Irish Poets* (Bloodaxe 2010). He lives in east London with his wife and son. He writes, 'I have a fairly strict rule that I don't talk about the meaning of my poems for the very good reason that what other people think they're about is invariably far more interesting than what I think they're about. However, at the risk of disappointing anyone who read this poem and took it to refer to the death, possibly by poisoning, of Louis X of France in 1316, I'll try to describe what I think it's getting at. I almost never have an idea of what I want to communicate before I start writing, I usually (though not always) find that out along the way, but on this occasion I did have something specific in mind. I wanted to talk about the sense I have that my decisions are made by an inner infant and not by my adult self who likes to imagine he's in charge.

'In the poem the maggot manipulates the adult fly's controls as though the maggot is a pilot and the fly body, his aircraft. The male maggot, who peers out of the fly body that surrounds him, then spies, through a crack in a female fly's body, her inner maggot. That glimpse is meant to represent a glimpse of a woman's sex organs (the maggots in the poem partly represent sexuality and they're described in a way that's meant to make them seem a bit genital). The rest of the poem mourns the repression of our outrageous (and beautiful) id-like maggots as they're subdued by the gathering constraints of adulthood. In the poem, the pupa is imagined as the maggot's coffin. The black fly that emerges from the pupa is dressed in mourning for the maggot who must henceforth live inside the black crate of exoskeleton and can only now be accessed sexually. I know these ideas almost certainly won't come across literally, but I hope something of the feeling that, for me, surrounds them might.'

RORY WATERMAN was born in Belfast in 1981, and grew up in Lincolnshire in eastern England. He currently lives in Bristol, and recently completed a PhD at the University of Leicester, where he teaches modern literature. His poems have appeared in *New Poetries V* (Carcanet, 2011) and various other publications, and his first collection, *Tonight the Summer's Over*, is forthcoming with Carcanet in 2013. He co-edits *New Walk*, a magazine for poetry and the arts. He writes the following, 'I have always been drawn to small, peripheral islands. I suppose a lot of people are. Perhaps this is partly because they represent isolation and freedom, imprisonment and liberty, at the same time. To visit them is to flirt with a romantic impulse to break off. For me, as a child, this had an extra dimension. I grew up in rural Lincolnshire, which has a long and largely featureless coastline but nowhere near the inland villages I (happily) called home. However, my dad lived five miles from a ruggedy Irish coast, and not all that much further from Rathlin Island, with its ninety or so people, colonies of seabirds, potent lighthouses and eight square miles of turf surrounded by deadly currents and shipwrecks. My love of islands is almost obsessional, and perhaps Rathlin is to blame.

'But such small islands can have terrible histories: as much as they are peripheral, they also often mark strategic thresholds. In 1575, during the Enterprise of Ulster, Drake and Norreys had the 600 or so inhabitants of Rathlin put to the sword. It was hard to run away. Marstrand, today a far more developed island than somewhere like Rathlin, is home to a seventeenth-century fortress, built to defend Bohuslän from Norwegian attack after the Treaty of Roskilde, which had caused this border province to be ceded to Sweden. The fortress served another purpose, though, as my poem indicates. If the poem is about anything, it is this juxtaposition of freedom and imprisonment, the fallacy undermining some of our deepest – and truest – impulses, and how, when it comes down to it, we can't escape but we can be imprisoned. I hope it has other, modern resonances, too.'

SAMANTHA WYNNE-RHYDDERCH's second collection, *Not in These Shoes* was shortlisted for Wales Book of the Year 2009. Her third book, *Banjo* was published by Picador in June 2012. Samantha's poems have appeared in *Poetry Wales, Poetry London* and the *Forward Anthology 2002* and *2009*. In addition to a Hawthornden Fellowship she has received awards for her work from the Society of Authors (2007) and Literature Wales (1997 and 2002). Samantha is currently Leverhulme Poet in Residence at the National Museum of Wales. See www.rhydderch.com

She comments, 'Every time I visit Aberystwyth I cannot resist looking into *Craft*, a secondhand furniture shop that runs the length of the railway platform. It is one long room that morphs from hallway to lounge to bedroom, full of the discarded paraphernalia of the dead, with an anteroom bristling with mirrors, trinkets and the hard stare of china dogs. You don't have to rummage for long to discover tiny treasures for as little as twenty pence. Last year I bought a pair of miniature Delft clogs there and I started to think about all the Delftware that has been handed down through families or handed over to *Craft* as bric-à-brac. I began to wonder who had owned these objects, what they had meant to their owners and what such a present said about the relationship between recipient and donor. With this in mind, I started to reflect on using the Delft in a poem to articulate the speaker's relationship with a dead relative. Two lines into the poem I realised that I had begun writing against the backdrop of a flat where I'd lived on the fifth floor of a 19th century tenement in Paris. As soon as I imagined dropping a Delft figurine down these stairs, the crack that I heard opened up the poem and I was able to write the rest of it very quickly.'

YANG LIAN, a Chinese poet, was born in Switzerland, grew up in China and now lives in London. He has published eleven volumes of poetry. His work has been translated into more than twenty-five languages, and include *Yi*; *Where the Sea Stands Still*; *Concentric Circles*; *Riding Pisces: Poems from Five Collections*; and *Lee Valley Poems*. His works have been reviewed as "like MacDiarmid meets Rilke with Samurai sword drawn!" and "one of the most representative voices of Chinese literature". His latest publication in English was *Jade Ladder: Contemporary Chinese Poetry* (Bloodaxe, 2012), which he co-edited with W.N. Herbert and others. Among other prizes, he won the Nonino International Literature Prize 2012 and has been elected a board member of PEN International in 2008 and 2011.

He writes, 'This powerful, terrified face stares silently at you. It's made of bronze, the form is symmetrical, the look part human and part animal, but clearly with a supernatural power. It is Taotie, the most mysterious, odd but extremely exquisite design carved everywhere on bronzes made in the Shang Dynasty (16th–11th century BC). But, are these designs just decorations? Then, why do they watch us from all possible angles like God(s)? Looking back at them, one can feel her/his present is sucked in and swallowed by the timeless ancient. In Anyang of Henan province, the site of Yin, the capital of the late Shang dynasty (after 13th century BC), archaeologists found there were huge numbers of human sacrifices, at the same time as when the Chinese character-system suddenly began without any evidence of so-called prior "evolution". This ancient language has been used throughout the centuries and is still in use. When I arrived in Anyang that night, I couldn't help but jump into a taxi to run into the darkness of Yin, and feel that the Shang moon was still hanging above me. The poem is made up of questions and is about these questions; perhaps they are all we are so far.'

Translator Pascale Petit adds, 'I translated this poem after descending into the subterranean vault of the Shanghai Museum with Yang Lian. The curator of bronzes brought in a large Shang dynasty *taotie* cauldron. As it was slowly unwrapped, we saw that there was a demon carved in low relief on the front and back of the vessel. He had tripod legs and verdigris cloud motifs around and inside his face. These cauldrons were thought to have been used for cannibalistic rites, but no one knew for sure if *taotie* was a god who demanded human sacrifice, since other finds in the old capital of Yin (now known as Anyang) reveal an advanced civilisation with the rudiments of early Chinese characters. I have a special interest in prehistoric artefacts and in demons, so this poem was a delight to work on and try to render in English. I do not speak Mandarin so the translation was done by talking through each line with Lian.'

JANE YEH was born in America and has lived in the UK since 2001. Her first collection, *Marabou* (Carcanet, 2005), was shortlisted for the Whitbread, Forward, and Jerwood Aldeburgh prizes. Her second collection, *The Ninjas*, will be published by Carcanet in November 2012. She teaches creative writing at Kingston University and for the Arvon Foundation, and lives in London.

She comments, '"The Birds" is the third poem I wrote in a particular style I was experimenting with at the time, in which I was deliberately trying to do the opposite of whatever I usually did in a poem. Instead of two lines, each stanza had four lines; instead of first-person narration, the poem was written in the third person. Making each line a complete sentence, no matter how long or wordy, was also a departure for me. These changes in form seemed to lead, without conscious decision-making, to a new voice, plainer and more direct, and new subject matter (slightly surreal or fantastical). As far as content, I'm not very fond of the pastoral or of "nature poetry", but the strangeness of birds has always appealed to me – they look like little aliens. I wanted to convey something of this feeling without making them sound too cutesy. Generally, in my writing, I try to keep myself entertained, in hopes of possibly doing the same for readers. So this poem is meant as an entertainment, light or otherwise.'

LIST OF MAGAZINES

Agenda, The Wheelwrights,
Fletching Street, Mayfield
East Sussex TN20 6TL
Editor: Patricia McCarthy

Ambit, 17 Priory Gardens
London N6 5QY
Editor: Martin Bax

Blackbox Manifold, http://www.
manifold.group.shef.ac.uk/
Pembroke College, University of
Cambridge, Cambridge CB2 1RF
Editors: Alex Houen

Brand Magazine, www.
brandliterarymagazine.co.uk/
Editor: Nina Rapi

Brittle Star, PO Box 56108,
London E17 0AY
Editors: Louisa Hooper, Jacqueline
Gabbitas, David Floyd, Martin
Parker

Cambridge Literary Review,
Cambridge Literary Review
Trinity Hall, Cambridge CB2 1TJ
Editors: Boris Jardine & Lydia
Wilson

Clinic, http://clinicpresents.com/
Editors: Sam Buchan-Watts,
Andrew Parkes, Rachael Allen,
Sean Roy Parker

The Dark Horse, 3A Blantyre
Mill Road, Bothwell, South
Lanarkshire, G71 8DD
Editor: Gerry Cambridge

The Delinquent, www.
thedelinquent.co.uk/
92 Elm Road, Kingston, Surrey,
KT2 6HU
Editors: Jason King, Jeremy Quinn

Edinburgh Review, 22a Buccleuch
Place, Edinburgh EH8 9LN

Fuselit, www.fuselit.co.uk/
Editors: Kirsten Irving, Jon Stone

Halfcircle, www.halfcirclepoetry.
blogspot.co.uk/
Editor: Arabella Currie and
Thomas Graham

Horizon Review,
www.saltpublishing.com/horizon/
Editor: Katy Evans-Bush

London Review of Books
28 Little Russell Street, London
WC1A 2HN
Editors: Paul Myerscough,
Daniel Soar

Magma, www.magmapoetry.com/
23 Pine Walk, Carshalton
SM5 4ES

Modern Poetry in Translation
The Queens College, Oxford
OX1 4AW
Editor: Sasha Dugdale

New Linear Perspectives, www.
newlinearperspectives.wordpress.
com/
Editor Andrew F. Giles

New Welsh Review, PO Box 170, Aberystwyth, Ceredigion, SY23 1WZ
Editor: Gwen Davies

The North The Poetry Business Ltd., Bank Street Arts, 32–40 Bank Street, Sheffield S1 2DS
Editors: Ann Sansom and Peter Sansom

PN Review, Dept. of English, University of Glasgow, 5 University Gardens, Glasgow, G12 8QH
Editor: Michael Schmidt

The Poet's Calendar University of Chichester, College Lane, West Sussex, Chichester, PO19 6PE.
Editor: Diana Barsham

Poetry and Audience The School of English, University of Leeds, Leeds, West Yorkshire LS2 9JT
Editor: Amy Ramsay

Poetry London, 81 Lambeth Walk, London SE11 6DX
Editor: Colette Bryce

Poetry Review, The Poetry Society, 22 Betterton Street, London, WC2H 9BX

Poetry Wales, 57 Nolton Street, Bridgend, Wales, CF31 3AE UK
Editor: Zoë Skoulding

The Rialto, PO Box 309, Aylesham, Norwich NR11 6LN
Editor: Michael Mackmin

Stand The School of English, University of Leeds, Leeds, West Yorkshire LS2 9JT
Editors: John Whale and Elaine Glover

10th Muse, www.nonism.org.uk/muse.html
Editor: Andrew Jordan

13 Pages www.thirteenpages.wordpress.com/
Editors: Will Harris and Richard Osmond

The Warwick Review, Department of English, University of Warwick Coventry CV4 7AL
Editor Michael Hulse

The White Review, www.thewhitereview.org
8th Floor, 1 Knightsbridge Green, London SW1X 7QA
Editors: Benjamin Eastham and Jacques Testard

The Wolf, April Heights, Fagnal Lane, Winchmore Hill, Amersham HP7 0PG
Editor: James Byrne

ACKNOWLEDGEMENTS

Grateful acknowledgement is made to the publications from which the poems in this volume were chosen. Unless specifically noted otherwise, copyright to the poems is held by the individual poets.

Fleur Adcock: "Bees' Nest" appeared in *Poetry London*. Reprinted by permission of the poet.

Patience Agbabi: "Unfinished Business" appeared in *Poetry Review*. Reprinted by permission of the poet.

Tara Bergin: "Stag-Boy" appeared in *Modern Poetry in Translation*. Reprinted by permission of the poet.

Liz Berry: "Sow" appeared in *Poetry London*. Reprinted by permission of the poet.

Alison Brackenbury: "Roll-on" appeared in *The North*. Reprinted by permission of the poet.

Vahni Capildeo: "Four Departures from 'Wulf and Eadwacer'" appeared in *Blackbox Manifold*. Reprinted by permission of the poet.

Melanie Challenger: "Suilven or Humility" appeared in *Poetry and Audience*. Reprinted by permission of the poet.

Amarjit Chandan: "The Prisoner Being Released" appeared in *Modern Poetry in Translation*. Reprinted by permission of the poet.

Gillian Clarke: "Swans" appeared in *Magma*. Reprinted by permission of the poet.

John Wedgwood Clarke: "Sandside" appeared in *The Wolf*. Reprinted by permission of the poet.

John Clegg: "Mermaids" appeared in *Horizon Review*. Reprinted by permission of the poet.

David Constantine: "A Local Habitation" appeared in *The Rialto*. Reprinted by permission of the poet.

Sarah Corbett: "An English Walk" appeared in *Poetry Review*. Reprinted by permission of the poet.

Abi Curtis: "Purpose-Built Town" appeared in *Ambit*. Reprinted by permission of the poet.

Amy De'Ath: "Failure" appeared in *Halfcircle*. Reprinted by permission of the poet.

Christine De Luca: "Discontinuity" appeared in *The Dark Horse*. Reprinted by permission of the poet.

Michael Egan: "intermission" appeared in *10th Muse*. Reprinted by permission of the poet.

Elaine Feinstein: "Damage" appeared in *PN Review*. Reprinted by permission of the poet.

Jane Flett: "This Cowgirl's Lament" appeared in *The Delinquent*. Reprinted by permission of the poet.

John Gallas: "from pacifications" appeared in *PN Review*. Reprinted by permission of the poet.

John Gohorry: "from Keeping the City" appeared in *The Warwick Review*. Reprinted by permission of the poet.

Andrew Greig: "Wynd" appeared in *Edinburgh Review* and is collected in *As Though We Were Flying* (Bloodaxe, 2011). Reprinted by permission of the poet and the publisher.

Vona Groarke: "Midsummer" appeared in *Poetry London*. Reprinted by permission of the poet.

Jo Haslam: "Hart" appeared in *The Rialto*. Reprinted by permission of the poet.

Michael Haslam: "Old Lad" appeared in *Cambridge Literary Review*. Reprinted by permission of the poet.

Paul Henry: "Usk" appeared in *Poetry Wales*. Reprinted by permission of the poet.

Selima Hill: "The Elephant Whose Sturgeon-like Blood" appeared in *Poetry London*. Reprinted by permission of the poet.

Sheila Hillier: "Re-entry" appeared in *Brittle Star*. Reprinted by permission of the poet.

Sarah Howe: "Death of Orpheus" appeared in *The White Review*. Reprinted by permission of the poet.

Joanna Ingham: "The Corpse Road" appeared in *Ambit*. Reprinted by permission of the poet.

Anthony Joseph: "River Dove" appeared in *Brand* and was collected in *Rubber Orchestras* (Salt, 2011) Reprinted by permission of the poet and publisher.

Annie Katchinska: "Tawpie" appeared in *Poetry London*. Reprinted by permission of the poet.

David Kinloch: "from I, Giraffe" appeared in *PN Review*. Reprinted by permission of the poet.

Janet Kofi-Tsekpo: "The Arch" appeared in *PN Review*. Reprinted by permission of the poet.

Tim Liardet: "Deleted Scene (The Frog)" appeared in *Agenda*. Reprinted by permission of the poet.

Frances Leviston: "A Shrunken Head" appeared in *London Review of Books*. Reprinted by permission of the poet.

Fran Lock: "from The Mystic and The Pig Thief" appeared in *Poetry London*. Reprinted by permission of the poet.

Richie McCaffery: "Ballast Flint" appeared in *New Linear Perspectives*. Reprinted by permission of the poet.

Karen McCarthy Woolf: "Old Mutha Riah. Hoxton 1935" appeared in *Modern Poetry in Translation*. Reprinted by permission of the poet.

Jamie McKendrick: "King Billy's Nemesis" appeared in *Poetry London*. Reprinted by permission of the poet.

Michael McKimm: "Water Cure" appeared in *The Warwick Review*. Reprinted by permission of the poet.

Hugh McMillan: "Too Big a Part" appeared in *The Rialto*. Reprinted by permission of the poet.

Kathryn Maris: "What Will Happen To The Neighbours When The Earth Floods?" appeared in *New Welsh Review*. Reprinted by permission of the poet.

Hilary Menos: "Bob's Dogs" appeared in *New Welsh Review*. Reprinted by permission of the poet.

Harriet Moore: "Bog Bodies" appeared in *Clinic*. Reprinted by permission of the poet.

Kim Moore: "The Drowned Fields" appeared in *Clinic*. Reprinted by permission of the poet.

David Morley: "Ballad of the Moon, Moon" appeared in *Modern Poetry in Translation*. Reprinted by permission of the poet.

Graham Mort: "Passed" appeared in *The Rialto* and is collected in *Cusp* (Seren, 2011) Reprinted by permission of the poet and the publisher.

Stephanie Norgate: "Free style" appeared in *The Poet's Calendar*. Reprinted by permission of the poet.

Bernard O'Donoghue: "Sardines" appeared in *13 Pages*. Reprinted by permission of the poet.

Richard Owens: "Immigrant Song" appeared in *Poetry Wales*. Reprinted by permission of the poet.

Ruth Padel: "Ripples on New Grass" appeared in *London Review of Books* and is collected in *The Mara Crossing* (Chatto & Windus, 2012) Reprinted by permission of the poet and the publisher.

Alasdair Paterson: "Pomegranate" appeared in *Stand* and was collected in *Brumaire and Later* (Flarestack Poets, 2011). Reprinted by permission of the poet and the publisher.

Anita Pati: "An unborn child wonders if it's worth it" appeared in *Magma*. Reprinted by permission of the poet.

Eleanor Perry: "Sole" appeared in *The Delinquent*. Reprinted by permission of the poet.

Pascale Petit: "Notre Dame Father" appeared in *Magma*. Reprinted by permission of the poet.

Jacob Polley: "Lunarian" appeared in *13 Pages*. Reprinted by permission of the poet.

Caroline Price: "After" appeared in *The North*. Reprinted by permission of the poet.

Anne Rouse: "High Wall" appeared in *Poetry Review*. Reprinted by permission of the poet.

Kathryn Simmonds: "Experience" appeared in *Poetry Review*. Reprinted by permission of the poet.

Zoë Skoulding: "The Man in the Moone" appeared in *PN Review*. Reprinted by permission of the poet.

Linus Slug: "wulmonath" appeared in *Cambridge Literary Review*. Reprinted by permission of the poet.

Anne Stevenson: "It's astonishing" appeared in *Poetry Review*. Reprinted by permission of the poet.

Greta Stoddart: "The Curtain" appeared in *Poetry London*. Reprinted by permission of the poet.

Claire Trévien: "Sing Bird" appeared in *Fuselit*. Reprinted by permission of the poet.

Mark Waldron: "The Life Cycle of the Fly" appeared in *Poetry London*. Reprinted by permission of the poet.

Rory Waterman: "Marstrand" appeared in *Stand*. Reprinted by permission of the poet.

Samantha Wynne-Rhydderch: "Delft" appeared in *Magma*. Reprinted by permission of the poet.

Yang Lian: "Questions about the Demon Taotie" appeared in *Poetry Review*. Reprinted by permission of the poet.

Jane Yeh: "The Birds" appeared in *PN Review*. Reprinted by permission of the poet.